# Contents

# Introduction

Welcome to **" Trivia for Seniors: 500 Multiple-Choice Questions from the 1950s to the 1990s "**!
This book is much more than a collection of questions; it's a journey through some of the most vibrant and influential decades of our time. Whether you're a baby boomer, a fan of retro culture, or simply someone who loves to test their knowledge of history, this book is designed to bring joy, challenge, and a sense of nostalgia.

As we age, keeping our minds active and engaged is crucial for our overall well-being. Engaging with trivia and memory games is a fantastic way to keep our brains sharp, improve our memory recall, and even learn something new along the way. This book focuses on the events, music, movies, sports, and significant happenings from the 1950s to the 1990s, offering a delightful mix of entertainment and cognitive stimulation.

Each section of the book is dedicated to a different decade, starting with the 1950s and moving through to the 1990s. You'll find 100 multiple-choice questions in each section, designed to be both challenging and fun. And don't worry if you can't remember everything – the answers are provided at the back of the book.

But this book isn't just about testing your memory. It's also about rekindling those precious moments from the past. At the end of each section, you'll find a "My Memory" page where you're encouraged to jot down your personal memories and stories from each era. It's a wonderful way to reflect on your life experiences and share them with friends, family, or fellow trivia enthusiasts.

So, whether you're looking to challenge yourself, take a walk down memory lane, or simply enjoy some light-hearted entertainment, this book is the perfect companion. Grab a cup of coffee, settle into your favorite chair, and get ready to explore the rich history and fun memories that each decade has to offer!

Happy quizzing!

# How to Use This Book

Getting Started

This trivia book is designed to be simple and enjoyable to use. You don't need any special tools or knowledge – just a willingness to dive into the questions and perhaps a pen or pencil if you'd like to note your answers or record personal memories.

Answering the Questions

- **Read Each Question Carefully**: Each question has been crafted to challenge and entertain. Take your time reading through them.
- **Choose Your Answer**: For each question, there are four choices (A, B, C, and D). Select the answer you think is correct. You can mark your choice directly in the book or use a separate sheet of paper if you plan to share the book with others.
- **No Time Limit**: There's no rush to complete the questions. Feel free to take breaks and come back to where you left off.

Checking Your Answers

- At the end of each decade section, you'll find the answers to all the questions in that section.
- Check your answers and tally your score if you wish. This can be a fun way to track your progress or turn the activity into a friendly competition with others.

Using the "My Memory" Pages

- After each set of trivia questions, you'll find a "My Memory" page. This is your space to reflect and write.
- Feel free to jot down any personal stories, memories, or thoughts that the questions from each decade bring up. This can be a wonderful way to connect the past with the present and share experiences with others.

Enjoying the Experience

- Remember, this book is as much about enjoying the journey through the decades as it is about getting the answers right.
- Feel free to use this book in group settings, like family gatherings or social groups, as a fun and engaging way to spark conversations and share memories.

Keeping Your Brain Active

- Regularly engaging with the trivia questions in this book can be a great way to keep your mind sharp and active.
- Challenge yourself to answer a few questions each day, or set aside time each week for a trivia session.

We hope you find "Trivia for Seniors: 500 Multiple-Choice Memorable 50s-90s Events Questions and Answers" both enjoyable and stimulating. Happy reminiscing and good luck with your trivia adventure!

# Section 1: The 1950s

Welcome to the Fabulous Fifties!

Step into the world of the 1950s, a decade marked by post-war prosperity, groundbreaking cultural shifts, and the birth of rock 'n' roll. It was a time of significant change and innovation, setting the stage for many of the societal transformations that would define the latter half of the 20th century. In this section, we'll explore a variety of topics from this dynamic decade, including politics, entertainment, sports, and key historical events.

## 1950s Trivia Questions

1. **Who was the President of the United States at the beginning of the 1950s?**
   A. Harry S. Truman
   B. Dwight D. Eisenhower
   C. John F. Kennedy
   D. Franklin D. Roosevelt

2. **Which movie, released in 1955, starred James Dean as a troubled teenager?**
   A. Rebel Without a Cause
   B. East of Eden
   C. Giant
   D. The Wild One

3. **What was the name of the first artificial Earth satellite, launched by the Soviet Union in 1957?**
   A. Sputnik 1
   B. Apollo 11
   C. Voyager 1
   D. Explorer 1

4. **In 1954, the U.S. Supreme Court ruled in which case that racial segregation in public schools was unconstitutional?**
   A. Plessy v. Ferguson
   B. Brown v. Board of Education
   C. Roe v. Wade
   D. Marbury v. Madison

5. **Which iconic Disney theme park opened in 1955?**

A. Walt Disney World
B. Disneyland
C. Disney Tokyo
D. Euro Disney

6. **What was the best-selling novel of the 1950s, written by Grace Metalious?**
A. To Kill a Mockingbird
B. Peyton Place
C. The Catcher in the Rye
D. Lord of the Flies

7. **Which war began in 1950 and ended in 1953?**
A. World War II
B. Vietnam War
C. Korean War
D. The Suez Crisis

8. **Who wrote the groundbreaking play 'Death of a Salesman' which premiered in 1949 and won the Pulitzer Prize in 1950?**
A. Tennessee Williams
B. Arthur Miller
C. Eugene O'Neill
D. Edward Albee

9. **In 1953, who became the first woman to reach the summit of Mount Everest?**
A. Junko Tabei
B. Mary Anderson
C. Sir Edmund Hillary
D. Tenzing Norgay

10. **Which iconic rock 'n' roll artist released "Heartbreak Hotel" in 1956?**

A. Chuck Berry
B. Elvis Presley
C. Buddy Holly
D. Little Richard

11. **Who was the famous blonde bombshell actress and sex symbol of the 1950s?**
A. Audrey Hepburn
B. Elizabeth Taylor
C. Marilyn Monroe
D. Grace Kelly

12. **What was the first color television show to be broadcast in the USA in 1951?**
A. I Love Lucy
B. The Ed Sullivan Show
C. The Lone Ranger
D. Rose Parade

13. **Which Alfred Hitchcock film, released in 1954, starred James Stewart and Grace Kelly?**
A. Vertigo
B. Rear Window
C. Psycho
D. North by Northwest

14. **In 1952, who became the Prime Minister of the United Kingdom, serving until 1955?**
A. Clement Attlee
B. Harold Macmillan
C. Winston Churchill

D. Anthony Eden

15. **What was the name of the first successful vaccine for polio, announced in 1955?**
A. Sabin Vaccine
B. Jonas Salk Vaccine
C. Pasteur Vaccine
D. Banting Vaccine

16. **Who wrote 'The Old Man and the Sea', which won the Pulitzer Prize for Fiction in 1953?**
A. Ernest Hemingway
B. William Faulkner
C. John Steinbeck
D. F. Scott Fitzgerald

17. **Which actress won an Academy Award for her performance in the 1954 film 'The Country Girl'?**
A. Audrey Hepburn
B. Katharine Hepburn
C. Grace Kelly
D. Elizabeth Taylor

18. **What was the popular dance craze that originated in the 1950s?**
A. The Twist
B. The Jitterbug
C. The Cha-Cha
D. Rock 'n' Roll

19. **Which groundbreaking sitcom first aired in 1951, featuring a Cuban bandleader and his zany wife?**
A. The Honeymooners
B. Leave It to Beaver
C. I Love Lucy
D. Father Knows Best

20. **The first NATO Secretary General, appointed in 1952, was from which country?**
A. United States
B. United Kingdom
C. France
D. Canada

21. **Which famous novel by J.D. Salinger, a classic of teenage rebellion, was published in 1951?**
A. On The Road
B. To Kill a Mockingbird
C. The Catcher in the Rye
D. Fahrenheit 451

22. **In 1958, NASA was established in response to the space race with which country?**
A. Germany
B. Soviet Union
C. China
D. Japan

23. **Which iconic figure won four gold medals in the 1956 Melbourne Olympics,**

revolutionizing swimming with his techniques?
A. Johnny Weissmuller
B. Mark Spitz
C. Michael Phelps
D. Murray Rose

24. **What was the name of the first commercially successful video tape recorder, released in 1956?**
A. Betamax
B. VHS
C. Ampex
D. Video 2000

25. **Which 1954 Supreme Court case ended 'separate but equal' in public education in the United States?**
A. Miranda v. Arizona
B. Brown v. Board of Education
C. Roe v. Wade
D. Plessy v. Ferguson

26. **Who was the first African American to win an Academy Award, doing so in 1950?**
A. Sidney Poitier
B. Dorothy Dandridge
C. Hattie McDaniel
D. James Baskett

27. **What genre of music, combining elements of gospel and rhythm and blues, became popular in the 1950s?**
A. Rock 'n' Roll

B. Jazz

C. Disco

D. Country

28. **Which 1950 film, starring Gloria Swanson and William Holden, is about a fading silent film star and a young screenwriter?**

A. All About Eve

B. A Streetcar Named Desire

C. Sunset Boulevard

D. Singin' in the Rain

29. **Who became the leader of the Soviet Union in 1953 after the death of Joseph Stalin?**

A. Leonid Brezhnev

B. Nikita Khrushchev

C. Mikhail Gorbachev

D. Vladimir Lenin

30. **In 1959, which state became the 50th state of the United States?**

A. Alaska

B. Hawaii

C. Puerto Rico

D. Guam

31. **Which popular TV show, featuring a suburban housewife and her Cuban-American husband, first aired in 1951?**

A. The Honeymooners

B. I Love Lucy

C. The Andy Griffith Show

D. Leave It to Beaver

32. **What was the landmark U.S. Supreme Court decision in 1954 that declared segregation in public schools unconstitutional?**
A. Roe v. Wade
B. Brown v. Board of Education
C. Miranda v. Arizona
D. Marbury v. Madison

33. **In 1958, who became the first person to orbit the Earth in space?**
A. Yuri Gagarin
B. Alan Shepard
C. John Glenn
D. None of the above; the first orbital flight was in 1961

34. **Which movie, released in 1959, starred Charlton Heston and won 11 Academy Awards?**
A. Spartacus
B. The Ten Commandments
C. Ben-Hur
D. Lawrence of Arabia

35. **Who was the American civil rights leader who led the Montgomery bus boycott in 1955?**
A. Malcolm X
B. Rosa Parks
C. Martin Luther King Jr.
D. Frederick Douglass

36. **Which novel, considered a classic of modern American literature, was published by Jack Kerouac in 1957?**
A. Invisible Man
B. On the Road
C. To Kill a Mockingbird
D. Catch-22

37. **In 1950, which country invaded South Korea, leading to the Korean War?**
A. China
B. Soviet Union
C. North Korea
D. Japan

38. **What was the name of the first credit card, introduced in 1950?**
A. American Express
B. MasterCard
C. Visa
D. Diners Club

39. **Which British expedition, in 1953, successfully reached the summit of Mount Everest for the first time?**
A. Edmund Hillary and Tenzing Norgay
B. George Mallory and Andrew Irvine
C. Chris Bonington and Doug Scott
D. Reinhold Messner and Peter Habeler

40. **In 1956, Elvis Presley made his first appearance on which famous TV show?**
A. The Ed Sullivan Show
B. The Tonight Show

C. American Bandstand

D. The Milton Berle Show

41.    **Which iconic American actress and model, known for playing "dumb blonde" characters, achieved fame in the 1950s?**

A. Audrey Hepburn

B. Elizabeth Taylor

C. Marilyn Monroe

D. Grace Kelly

42.    **The 1952 Winter Olympics were held in which European city?**

A. Innsbruck, Austria

B. Oslo, Norway

C. Cortina d'Ampezzo, Italy

D. St. Moritz, Switzerland

43.    **In 1957, which musical by Leonard Bernstein and Stephen Sondheim debuted on Broadway, becoming a huge hit?**

A. Guys and Dolls

B. West Side Story

C. My Fair Lady

D. The Sound of Music

44.    **Which American author won the Nobel Prize in Literature in 1954?**

A. John Steinbeck

B. Ernest Hemingway

C. William Faulkner

D. F. Scott Fitzgerald

45.    **The first successful polio vaccine was developed by which scientist in 1955?**

A. Albert Sabin
B. Jonas Salk
C. Louis Pasteur
D. Alexander Fleming

46. **What was the title of the first animated feature film to be released in widescreen Cinemascope, in 1959?**
A. Peter Pan
B. Cinderella
C. Sleeping Beauty
D. Snow White and the Seven Dwarfs

47. **In 1954, which Asian country won independence from France after the Battle of Dien Bien Phu?**
A. Vietnam
B. Cambodia
C. Laos
D. Thailand

48. **Which American play, considered a masterpiece of theater, debuted in 1955 and was written by Tennessee Williams?**
A. A Streetcar Named Desire
B. Cat on a Hot Tin Roof
C. The Glass Menagerie
D. The Crucible

49. **Who was the first African-American woman to win a Grand Slam title in tennis, achieving this in 1956?**
A. Serena Williams
B. Althea Gibson

C. Venus Williams
D. Billie Jean King

50. **The Treaty of Rome, which laid the foundation for the European Union, was signed in what year of the 1950s?**
A. 1950
B. 1955
C. 1957
D. 1959

51. **Which popular children's book, featuring a mischievous cat in a hat, was published by Dr. Seuss in 1957?**
A. Green Eggs and Ham
B. The Cat in the Hat
C. Horton Hears a Who!
D. One Fish Two Fish Red Fish Blue Fish

52. **In 1951, which African American singer became the first to perform at the Metropolitan Opera in New York City?**
A. Ella Fitzgerald
B. Billie Holiday
C. Marian Anderson
D. Sarah Vaughan

53. **Which landmark U.S. Supreme Court case in 1952 affirmed the right of the president to seize private property during a national emergency?**
A. Brown v. Board of Education
B. Youngstown Sheet & Tube Co. v. Sawyer
C. Roe v. Wade

D. Miranda v. Arizona

54. **What was the first feature-length animated movie produced by Walt Disney to be released in the 1950s?**
A. Cinderella
B. Snow White and the Seven Dwarfs
C. Sleeping Beauty
D. Peter Pan

55. **The novel 'Lolita', which later became a controversial classic, was first published in 1955 by which author?**
A. J.D. Salinger
B. Ernest Hemingway
C. Vladimir Nabokov
D. F. Scott Fitzgerald

56. **In 1958, which toy, a simple plastic hoop, became a huge fad among children and adults alike?**
A. Yo-Yo
B. Frisbee
C. Slinky
D. Hula Hoop

57. **Which country's revolution in 1959 led to Fidel Castro becoming its leader?**
A. Brazil
B. Mexico
C. Cuba
D. Venezuela

58.     The 'Golden Age of Television' in the 1950s saw the rise of which style of TV programming?
A. Sitcoms
B. Soap Operas
C. Game Shows
D. Live Television Dramas

59.     Which iconic American figure, known for his 'I Have a Dream' speech, became prominent in the civil rights movement during the late 1950s?
A. Malcolm X
B. Rosa Parks
C. Martin Luther King Jr.
D. Thurgood Marshall

60.     The 1956 Suez Crisis involved the nationalization of the Suez Canal by which country?
A. Israel
B. United Kingdom
C. France
D. Egypt

61.     Which popular board game, simulating property trading and management, was patented in 1955?
A. Risk
B. Monopoly
C. Scrabble
D. Clue

62.     **In 1954, Roger Bannister became the first person to run a mile in under how many minutes?**
A. Four minutes
B. Five minutes
C. Six minutes
D. Three minutes

63.     **Which actress starred in the Alfred Hitchcock classic 'Vertigo', released in 1958?**
A. Grace Kelly
B. Audrey Hepburn
C. Kim Novak
D. Ingrid Bergman

64.     **The 1952 Helsinki Olympics were notable for the debut of which Soviet athlete, known as the 'Russian Bear'?**
A. Vladimir Kuts
B. Emil Zátopek
C. Aleksandr Karelin
D. Valery Brumel

65.     **Which 1959 animated film by Disney featured a sleeping princess and an evil fairy?**
A. Cinderella
B. Snow White and the Seven Dwarfs
C. Sleeping Beauty
D. The Little Mermaid

66. **Who became the Prime Minister of India in 1950, following the assassination of Mahatma Gandhi?**
A. Indira Gandhi
B. Jawaharlal Nehru
C. Lal Bahadur Shastri
D. Rajendra Prasad

67. **What popular TV western series, starting in 1955, featured the Cartwright family?**
A. Gunsmoke
B. Bonanza
C. The Lone Ranger
D. The Rifleman

68. **Which car model, introduced by Chevrolet in 1953, became an iconic American sports car?**
A. Ford Mustang
B. Chevrolet Corvette
C. Dodge Charger
D. Pontiac GTO

69. **The Treaty of San Francisco, formally ending World War II with Japan, was signed in what year of the 1950s?**
A. 1950
B. 1951
C. 1952
D. 1953

70.    **Which famous American musician, known as 'The King of Rock and Roll', was drafted into the U.S. Army in 1958?**
A. Chuck Berry
B. Jerry Lee Lewis
C. Elvis Presley
D. Buddy Holly

71.    **In 1950, what was the name of the first Peanuts comic strip by Charles M. Schulz?**
A. Snoopy
B. Charlie Brown
C. Lucy
D. Peanuts

72.    **Which iconic film starring Marilyn Monroe and featuring the song 'Diamonds Are a Girl's Best Friend' was released in 1953?**
A. Some Like It Hot
B. The Seven Year Itch
C. How to Marry a Millionaire
D. Gentlemen Prefer Blondes

73.    **The 1958 World's Fair, known for showcasing technology and culture, was held in which city?**
A. New York
B. Brussels
C. Paris
D. London

74.    **Which U.S. state was admitted as the 49th state in 1959?**

A. Alaska
B. Hawaii
C. California
D. Arizona

75. **Who was the British Prime Minister at the start of the 1950s, known for his leadership during World War II?**
A. Clement Attlee
B. Winston Churchill
C. Anthony Eden
D. Harold Macmillan

76. **What type of music, characterized by a strong backbeat and electric guitars, became increasingly popular in the 1950s?**
A. Jazz
B. Blues
C. Rock 'n' Roll
D. Country

77. **Which famous American actress won an Academy Award for her performance in 'The Country Girl' (1954)?**
A. Audrey Hepburn
B. Grace Kelly
C. Elizabeth Taylor
D. Vivien Leigh

78. **In 1956, which canal was nationalized by Egypt, leading to an international crisis?**
A. Panama Canal
B. Suez Canal
C. Kiel Canal

D. Erie Canal

79.     **Which science fiction television series, created by Rod Serling, debuted in 1959?**
A. Star Trek
B. Doctor Who
C. The Twilight Zone
D. The Outer Limits

80.     **The first successful vaccine for polio was developed and announced in 1955 by which medical researcher?**
A. Albert Sabin
B. Jonas Salk
C. Alexander Fleming
D. Louis Pasteur

81.     **Which iconic American musical, featuring rival gangs in New York City, premiered on Broadway in 1957?**
A. Guys and Dolls
B. My Fair Lady
C. West Side Story
D. The Music Man

82.     **In 1959, which country experienced a successful revolution led by Fidel Castro?**
A. Mexico
B. Venezuela
C. Brazil
D. Cuba

83.     **What groundbreaking medical achievement occurred in 1954, involving Ronald Herrick and Richard Herrick?**

A. The first successful heart transplant
B. The discovery of the DNA double helix
C. The first successful kidney transplant
D. The development of the first polio vaccine

84.     **Who became the dominant figure in Soviet politics after Stalin's death in 1953?**
A. Leonid Brezhnev
B. Nikita Khrushchev
C. Mikhail Gorbachev
D. Vladimir Lenin

85.     **The popular TV series 'Gunsmoke', which began in 1955, was set in which fictional town?**
A. Laramie
B. Tombstone
C. Dodge City
D. Deadwood

86.     **Which 1954 movie, starring Marlon Brando, focused on mob violence and corruption on the waterfront?**
A. A Streetcar Named Desire
B. The Wild One
C. On the Waterfront
D. The Godfather

87.     **In 1952, who became the first African American to play in the Major Leagues for the Washington Senators?**
A. Jackie Robinson
B. Satchel Paige
C. Hank Aaron

D. Carlos Paula

**88.     What iconic Disneyland attraction, taking guests on a scenic boat tour, opened in 1955?**

A. Space Mountain

B. It's a Small World

C. Pirates of the Caribbean

D. Jungle Cruise

**89.     Which best-selling novel by Nevil Shute, depicting the aftermath of a nuclear war, was published in 1957?**

A. Alas, Babylon

B. On the Beach

C. The Chrysalids

D. A Canticle for Leibowitz

**90.     Which American actress and princess of Monaco retired from acting in 1956?**

A. Audrey Hepburn

B. Elizabeth Taylor

C. Grace Kelly

D. Marilyn Monroe

**91.     Which novel by William Golding about a group of boys stranded on an uninhabited island was published in 1954?**

A. Lord of the Flies

B. The Catcher in the Rye

C. Animal Farm

D. To Kill a Mockingbird

**92.     In 1955, who became the first African American to win an Emmy Award?**

A. Sidney Poitier
B. Ethel Waters
C. Dorothy Dandridge
D. Hattie McDaniel

93.     **The iconic American drama film 'Rebel Without a Cause', starring James Dean, was released in what year?**
A. 1953
B. 1954
C. 1955
D. 1956

94.     **Which American actress won an Academy Award for her leading role in the 1953 film 'Roman Holiday'?**
A. Grace Kelly
B. Audrey Hepburn
C. Elizabeth Taylor
D. Vivien Leigh

95.     **The famous Le Mans disaster, one of the worst accidents in motorsport history, occurred in what year of the 1950s?**
A. 1950
B. 1952
C. 1955
D. 1958

96.     **In 1950, which country was the first to declare its intention to boycott the Moscow Summer Olympics?**
A. United States
B. United Kingdom

C. Germany

D. None, as the Moscow Olympics were in 1980

97.     **Which science fiction novel by Ray Bradbury, set in a dystopian society where books are banned, was published in 1953?**

A. 1984

B. Brave New World

C. Fahrenheit 451

D. Atlas Shrugged

98.     **The first successful organ transplant, performed in 1954, was of which organ?**

A. Heart

B. Liver

C. Kidney

D. Lung

99.     **Which Broadway musical by Rodgers and Hammerstein, set in the South Pacific during WWII, won 10 Tony Awards in 1950?**

A. Oklahoma!

B. The Sound of Music

C. South Pacific

D. The King and I

100.     **In 1956, the popular TV quiz show 'Twenty-One' became infamous for what reason?**

A. Its long run of over a decade

B. The use of celebrity contestants

C. A major scandal involving rigged outcomes

D. Its innovative use of technology

# Memories from the 1950s

*Your stories and experiences from the 1950s:*

# The 1950s Word Search Challenge

```
W G Z K Z A B U C V D N C V F
J J L Z I S K C T N C I U T Q
P Q A P R N O L A I V E W O E
X J H M X R T L U W H V Y Q J
C U J D V X Y U P C A I C E M
N Y E E I E I B P Y B R S E T
X A T Y N R P P Y S K D C E E
Y T T S B K R O C K N R O L L
E K I O D I D L O V O G E C E
E D H N D N S I Z H K I N D V
F W I O G T H O I S A K K A I
S I V L E A Y K P Y I L L E S
I W A V H E E G V O V Q U I I
Y E F C U B R A W D L O C H O
P O O D L E S K I R T O W F N
```

| Beatnik | PoodleSkirt | Rocknroll | DriveIn |
|---------|-------------|-----------|---------|
| Cuba | Sputnik | NATO | Ike |
| Elvis | Disneyland | Television | Polio |
| Jazz | HulaHoop | Corvette | ColdWar |

# Section 2: The 1960s

A Decade of Transformation

Welcome to the 1960s – a decade marked by monumental shifts in politics, civil rights, music, and technology. From the space race to the rise of counterculture, the 1960s were a time of both turmoil and groundbreaking progress. In this section, we dive into the events that shaped this pivotal decade, exploring everything from the Vietnam War and the Civil Rights Movement to the Beatles and the moon landing.

# 1960s Trivia Questions

1. **Who became the President of the United States after the assassination of John F. Kennedy in 1963?**
   A. Lyndon B. Johnson
   B. Richard Nixon
   C. Gerald Ford
   D. Dwight D. Eisenhower

2. **Which historic event, a major step in the civil rights movement, occurred in Washington D.C. in August 1963?**
   A. Signing of the Civil Rights Act
   B. The March on Washington
   C. The Stonewall Riots
   D. The Watts Riots

3. **What was the name of the first human spaceflight program by the United States, announced in 1961?**
   A. Apollo Program
   B. Gemini Program
   C. Mercury Program
   D. Skylab Program

4. **Which British rock band, formed in 1960, became one of the most influential bands of all time?**
   A. The Rolling Stones
   B. The Beatles
   C. Pink Floyd
   D. The Who

5. **In 1964, which U.S. civil rights leader won the Nobel Peace Prize?**
   A. Malcolm X
   B. Rosa Parks
   C. Martin Luther King Jr.
   D. Thurgood Marshall
6. **The Cuban Missile Crisis, a major event of the Cold War, took place in what year?**
   A. 1960
   B. 1961
   C. 1962
   D. 1963
7. **Which book by Betty Friedan, published in 1963, is often credited with sparking the second wave of feminism in the United States?**
   A. The Feminine Mystique
   B. Sexual Politics
   C. The Second Sex
   D. The Female Eunuch
8. **What was the name of the American music festival in 1969 that became an emblem of the counterculture movement?**
   A. Monterey Pop Festival
   B. Altamont Free Concert
   C. Woodstock
   D. Isle of Wight Festival
9. **Which amendment to the United States Constitution, ratified in 1964, abolished poll taxes?**

A. 22nd Amendment
B. 24th Amendment
C. 26th Amendment
D. 27th Amendment

10. **Who was the first American astronaut to orbit the Earth, doing so in 1962?**
A. Neil Armstrong
B. Alan Shepard
C. John Glenn
D. Buzz Aldrin

11. **Which conflict escalated in the 1960s and became a major point of contention in U.S. foreign and domestic policy?**
A. The Korean War
B. The Vietnam War
C. The Cold War
D. The Cuban Missile Crisis

12. **The Beatles made their first appearance on The Ed Sullivan Show in what year?**
A. 1960
B. 1962
C. 1964
D. 1966

13. **In 1960, which African American author published 'To Kill a Mockingbird', a novel dealing with racial injustice?**
A. Maya Angelou
B. James Baldwin
C. Toni Morrison

D. Harper Lee

14.    **Which U.S. President declared the goal
of sending an American safely to the Moon
before the end of the 1960s?**
A. Dwight D. Eisenhower
B. Lyndon B. Johnson
C. John F. Kennedy
D. Richard Nixon

15.    **What was the name of the first
successful contraceptive pill, approved by
the FDA in 1960?**
A. Enovid
B. Ortho-Novum
C. Yasmin
D. Plan B

16.    **Which country gained independence
from Britain in 1960, becoming the Republic
of Cyprus?**
A. Malta
B. Cyprus
C. Singapore
D. Nigeria

17.    **The Civil Rights Act, which outlawed
discrimination based on race, color,
religion, sex, or national origin, was passed
in what year?**
A. 1960
B. 1964
C. 1965
D. 1968

18. In 1967, which city experienced one of the most severe instances of racial unrest in the United States, known as the '12th Street Riot'?
A. Los Angeles
B. New York
C. Chicago
D. Detroit

19. Which revolutionary book by Rachel Carson, published in 1962, led to the modern environmental movement?
A. The Sea Around Us
B. Walden
C. Silent Spring
D. The End of Nature

20. Who was the famous American boxer that won the World Heavyweight Championship in 1964 and later refused induction into the U.S. Army?
A. Joe Frazier
B. George Foreman
C. Sonny Liston
D. Muhammad Ali

21. Which landmark Supreme Court case in 1966 established the rights of criminal suspects, including the right to remain silent?
A. Brown v. Board of Education
B. Roe v. Wade

C. Miranda v. Arizona

D. Plessy v. Ferguson

22. **What famous wall, a symbol of the Cold War, was constructed in 1961?**

A. The Berlin Wall

B. The Great Wall of China

C. The Iron Curtain

D. The Israeli West Bank Barrier

23. **Which U.S. spacecraft successfully landed the first two astronauts on the Moon in 1969?**

A. Apollo 11

B. Apollo 13

C. Gemini 5

D. Mercury-Atlas 6

24. **In 1965, which march led by Martin Luther King Jr. was a pivotal moment in the Civil Rights Movement?**

A. The March on Washington

B. The Freedom Rides

C. The Selma to Montgomery March

D. The Chicago Freedom Movement

25. **Which famous music festival, known for its pivotal role in the counterculture movement, took place in 1969?**

A. Monterey Pop Festival

B. Woodstock

C. Altamont Free Concert

D. Isle of Wight Festival

26.      **What influential 1962 book by Michael Harrington helped to shed light on poverty in America?**
A. The Other America
B. The Affluent Society
C. The Culture of Poverty
D. The American Way of Poverty

27.      **In 1960, which country became the first in Africa to gain independence from colonial rule?**
A. Kenya
B. Nigeria
C. Ghana
D. South Africa

28.      **Who was the famous French New Wave director who released the film 'Breathless' in 1960?**
A. François Truffaut
B. Jean-Luc Godard
C. Claude Chabrol
D. Eric Rohmer

29.      **The Cuban Missile Crisis in 1962 was a 13-day confrontation between the United States and which other country?**
A. Cuba
B. China
C. Soviet Union
D. Vietnam

30. **Which African American activist and prominent figure in the Nation of Islam was assassinated in 1965?**
A. Martin Luther King Jr.
B. Malcolm X
C. Medgar Evers
D. Fred Hampton

31. **Which 1967 album by The Beatles is considered one of the most influential in music history, known for its psychedelic style and elaborate cover art?**
A. Abbey Road
B. Rubber Soul
C. Sgt. Pepper's Lonely Hearts Club Band
D. The White Album

32. **In 1961, which American astronaut became the first to travel into space, though not orbit the Earth?**
A. John Glenn
B. Alan Shepard
C. Gus Grissom
D. Neil Armstrong

33. **Which country's civil war, beginning in 1967 and ending in 1970, is known for the Biafran secessionist movement?**
A. Ethiopia
B. Congo
C. Nigeria
D. Angola

34.     In 1960, the U-2 incident involved an American spy plane being shot down over which country?
A. China
B. North Korea
C. Vietnam
D. Soviet Union

35.     **What name was given to the successful 1969 American campaign to land astronauts on the Moon?**
A. Operation Moonwalk
B. Project Apollo
C. Lunar Landing Mission
D. Space Race Victory

36.     **Which controversial book by Helen Gurley Brown, published in 1962, became a bestseller and sparked discussions about women's sexuality?**
A. The Feminine Mystique
B. The Female Eunuch
C. Sex and the Single Girl
D. Fear of Flying

37.     **In 1963, who became the first woman to travel into space, representing the Soviet Union?**
A. Sally Ride
B. Mae Jemison
C. Valentina Tereshkova
D. Judith Resnik

38.    **The Port Huron Statement, a manifesto of the student activist movement, was written in 1962 by members of which organization?**
A. The Black Panthers
B. The Weather Underground
C. Students for a Democratic Society (SDS)
D. The American Civil Liberties Union (ACLU)

39.    **Which influential 1963 film, directed by Stanley Kubrick, satirized the Cold War and nuclear scare?**
A. 2001: A Space Odyssey
B. The Shining
C. A Clockwork Orange
D. Dr. Strangelove

40.    **What was the major environmental disaster that struck the coast of Cornwall, England in 1967, leading to significant changes in maritime law?**
A. The Exxon Valdez oil spill
B. The Torrey Canyon oil spill
C. The Amoco Cadiz oil spill
D. The Prestige oil spill

41.    **Which American civil rights activist famously delivered the "I Have a Dream" speech during the March on Washington in 1963?**
A. Malcolm X
B. Rosa Parks
C. Martin Luther King Jr.

D. Thurgood Marshall

42. **The first episode of the iconic science fiction TV series 'Star Trek' aired in what year?**
A. 1963
B. 1964
C. 1966
D. 1969

43. **In 1968, which athlete made a symbolic protest against racial discrimination during the medal ceremony at the Mexico City Olympics?**
A. Muhammad Ali
B. Jesse Owens
C. Tommie Smith and John Carlos
D. Wilma Rudolph

44. **The 'Summer of Love', a social phenomenon that centered around the hippie culture, took place in which year?**
A. 1965
B. 1967
C. 1969
D. 1970

45. **Which amendment to the U.S. Constitution, ratified in 1967, established the procedure for presidential succession?**
A. 22nd Amendment
B. 23rd Amendment
C. 25th Amendment
D. 26th Amendment

46. **What was the title of the first James Bond film, released in 1962?**
A. Goldfinger
B. Dr. No
C. From Russia with Love
D. Thunderball

47. **In 1962, who became the first woman to be inducted into the Country Music Hall of Fame?**
A. Patsy Cline
B. Loretta Lynn
C. Kitty Wells
D. Tammy Wynette

48. **Which influential 1960 Hitchcock film, known for its shower scene, significantly impacted the thriller genre?**
A. Vertigo
B. North by Northwest
C. Psycho
D. The Birds

49. **Who founded the Black Panther Party in 1966?**
A. Malcolm X
B. Martin Luther King Jr.
C. Huey Newton and Bobby Seale
D. Angela Davis

50. **In 1964, which country hosted the Summer Olympics, becoming the first Asian country to do so?**
A. China

B. Japan
C. South Korea
D. Thailand

51.    **Which American author published 'In Cold Blood' in 1966, a pioneering work in the true crime genre?**
A. Truman Capote
B. Norman Mailer
C. Hunter S. Thompson
D. Jack Kerouac

52.    **The historic Freedom Rides, aimed at desegregating interstate bus travel, began in which year of the 1960s?**
A. 1960
B. 1961
C. 1963
D. 1965

53.    **In 1963, which British spy film, the third in its series, featured the iconic character James Bond?**
A. Goldfinger
B. From Russia with Love
C. Dr. No
D. Thunderball

54.    **Which famous concert by The Beatles, their last live performance, took place on the rooftop of Apple Records in 1969?**
A. Shea Stadium Concert
B. Cavern Club Concert
C. Hollywood Bowl Concert

D. The Rooftop Concert

55. **The Environmental Protection Agency (EPA) was established in the United States in what year of the 1960s?**
A. 1960
B. 1965
C. 1969
D. It was established in 1970

56. **In 1969, ARPANET, the precursor to the Internet, transmitted its first message between two computers located in which U.S. state?**
A. Massachusetts
B. New York
C. California
D. Texas

57. **Which landmark U.S. Supreme Court case in 1967 struck down state laws banning interracial marriage?**
A. Brown v. Board of Education
B. Roe v. Wade
C. Loving v. Virginia
D. Miranda v. Arizona

58. **In 1966, Mao Zedong launched the Cultural Revolution in which country?**
A. Vietnam
B. Korea
C. Japan
D. China

59.    **Which influential 1960s TV show, created by Gene Roddenberry, featured the USS Enterprise and its crew?**
A. Doctor Who
B. The Twilight Zone
C. Star Trek
D. Lost in Space

60.    **Who was the American civil rights leader, known for his philosophy of nonviolence and civil disobedience, assassinated in 1968?**
A. Malcolm X
B. Medgar Evers
C. Martin Luther King Jr.
D. Fred Hampton

61.    **The famous standoff known as the Cuban Missile Crisis occurred during the presidency of which U.S. President?**
A. Dwight D. Eisenhower
B. Lyndon B. Johnson
C. John F. Kennedy
D. Richard Nixon

62.    **In 1967, Kathrine Switzer became the first woman to officially run the Boston Marathon, despite which initial response?**
A. She was celebrated
B. She was ignored
C. She was disqualified
D. She was injured

63.     **Which pivotal 1960s event in the Civil Rights Movement occurred on the Edmund Pettus Bridge in Selma, Alabama?**
A. The Freedom Rides
B. The March on Washington
C. The Selma to Montgomery Marches
D. The Birmingham Campaign

64.     **The Beatles' album 'Revolver', which marked a significant evolution in their music style, was released in which year?**
A. 1965
B. 1966
C. 1967
D. 1968

65.     **In 1964, Sidney Poitier became the first African American to win an Academy Award for Best Actor for which film?**
A. Guess Who's Coming to Dinner
B. In the Heat of the Night
C. Lilies of the Field
D. To Sir, with Love

66.     **What was the name of the U.S. naval ship involved in an alleged attack that led to increased American involvement in the Vietnam War, known as the '______ Incident'?**
A. USS Arizona
B. USS Maine
C. USS Liberty
D. USS Maddox

67. **Which American author and poet, known for her book 'I Know Why the Caged Bird Sings', rose to prominence in the 1960s?**
A. Gwendolyn Brooks
B. Toni Morrison
C. Maya Angelou
D. Alice Walker

68. **In 1961, the United States sponsored an unsuccessful military invasion at the Bay of Pigs, aimed at overthrowing the government of which country?**
A. Vietnam
B. Cuba
C. Nicaragua
D. Iran

69. **The historic Apollo 11 mission, which resulted in the first human moon landing, took place in what year?**
A. 1967
B. 1968
C. 1969
D. 1970

70. **Which social movement, gaining significant momentum in the 1960s, focused on advocating for women's rights and equality?**
A. The Civil Rights Movement
B. The Anti-War Movement
C. The Feminist Movement
D. The Environmental Movement

71.     **Which landmark U.S. legislation, passed in 1965, removed discriminatory immigration quotas based on national origin?**
A. The Civil Rights Act
B. The Voting Rights Act
C. The Fair Housing Act
D. The Immigration and Nationality Act of 1965

72.     **In 1960, which country became the first in West Africa to gain independence from colonial rule?**
A. Nigeria
B. Ghana
C. Ivory Coast
D. Senegal

73.     **The first episode of the groundbreaking children's television show 'Sesame Street' aired in what year?**
A. 1966
B. 1969
C. 1971
D. 1973

74.     **What was the famous phrase spoken by Neil Armstrong as he stepped onto the Moon in 1969?**
A. "One small step for man, one giant leap for mankind."
B. "The Eagle has landed."
C. "Houston, Tranquility Base here."

D. "That's one step for a man, a giant leap for mankind."

75.     **Which best-selling self-help book by Dr. Benjamin Spock, influential in the 1960s, changed the way many parents raised their children?**
A. How to Win Friends and Influence People
B. The Feminine Mystique
C. The Power of Positive Thinking
D. The Common Sense Book of Baby and Child Care

76.     **The Peace Corps, a volunteer program run by the United States government, was established in which year of the 1960s?**
A. 1960
B. 1961
C. 1964
D. 1967

77.     **In 1968, student protests globally reached their peak, notably in which European country that experienced a major political crisis?**
A. Germany
B. United Kingdom
C. France
D. Italy

78.     **Which influential music festival in 1967, known as the first major rock festival, helped launch the careers of several major rock bands?**

A. Woodstock
B. Monterey Pop Festival
C. Altamont Free Concert
D. Isle of Wight Festival

79. **The historic Civil Rights Act of 1964 was signed into law by which U.S. President?**
A. John F. Kennedy
B. Richard Nixon
C. Lyndon B. Johnson
D. Dwight D. Eisenhower

80. **In 1964, who became the first African American to win the Nobel Peace Prize?**
A. Malcolm X
B. Medgar Evers
C. Martin Luther King Jr.
D. Ralph Bunche

81. **Which American band, formed in 1965 and known for hits like "Light My Fire", became one of the most iconic rock bands of the era?**
A. The Rolling Stones
B. The Beatles
C. Pink Floyd
D. The Doors

82. **The 'Hot Line', a direct communication link for emergency use, was established in 1963 between the leaders of the United States and which other country?**
A. China

B. Germany

C. Soviet Union

D. United Kingdom

83.      **In 1960, which country in Africa gained its independence from Belgium, leading to a significant political crisis?**

A. Rwanda

B. Burundi

C. Congo

D. Uganda

84.      **What was the name of the American spy plane pilot who was shot down and captured during a reconnaissance mission over the Soviet Union in 1960?**

A. John Glenn

B. Gary Powers

C. Chuck Yeager

D. Alan Shepard

85.      **In 1969, which Senator from Massachusetts was involved in a controversial car accident at Chappaquiddick Island?**

A. John F. Kennedy

B. Edward Kennedy

C. Robert F. Kennedy

D. Joseph P. Kennedy II

86.      **Which landmark 1966 Supreme Court case established the 'Miranda rights' of suspects in police custody?**

A. Brown v. Board of Education

B. Roe v. Wade
C. Miranda v. Arizona
D. Loving v. Virginia

87. **The first successful heart transplant was performed in 1967 by Dr. Christiaan Barnard in which country?**
A. United States
B. United Kingdom
C. South Africa
D. Australia

88. **Which 1968 science fiction film, directed by Stanley Kubrick, is renowned for its realistic depiction of space and its enigmatic narrative?**
A. 2001: A Space Odyssey
B. Star Wars
C. Blade Runner
D. The Day the Earth Stood Still

89. **Who was the influential fashion designer in the 1960s known for popularizing the miniskirt?**
A. Coco Chanel
B. Mary Quant
C. Vivienne Westwood
D. Yves Saint Laurent

90. **In 1966, Mao Zedong launched the Cultural Revolution, a campaign to reinforce communism by removing capitalist elements, in which country?**
A. Vietnam

B. Soviet Union

C. China

D. North Korea

91. **Which American activist and prominent figure in the Civil Rights Movement was assassinated in his own home in 1965?**

A. Martin Luther King Jr.

B. Malcolm X

C. Medgar Evers

D. Fred Hampton

92. **The Gulf of Tonkin Resolution, which escalated U.S. involvement in the Vietnam War, was passed in what year?**

A. 1962

B. 1964

C. 1966

D. 1968

93. **In 1963, Alfred Hitchcock released a horror-thriller film featuring aggressive and unexplained bird attacks. What was the title of this film?**

A. Psycho

B. Vertigo

C. The Birds

D. Rear Window

94. **Which spacecraft was the first to take humans to the moon, marking a significant milestone in the Space Race?**

A. Apollo 8

B. Apollo 11
C. Apollo 13
D. Gemini 3

95.    **In 1961, which country underwent a failed invasion at the Bay of Pigs, a significant event in the Cold War?**
A. Chile
B. Cuba
C. Brazil
D. Argentina

96.    **Which iconic music festival in 1969, remembered as a pinnacle of the hippie movement, was held at Max Yasgur's dairy farm?**
A. Monterey Pop Festival
B. Isle of Wight Festival
C. Woodstock
D. Altamont Free Concert

97.    **Who became the first female Prime Minister of Israel in 1969?**
A. Indira Gandhi
B. Margaret Thatcher
C. Golda Meir
D. Benazir Bhutto

98.    **Which amendment to the U.S. Constitution, ratified in 1964, prohibited the use of poll taxes in federal elections?**
A. 22nd Amendment
B. 24th Amendment
C. 26th Amendment

D. 27th Amendment

99.      **In 1967, Christiaan Barnard performed the world's first human heart transplant in which city?**
A. Johannesburg
B. Cape Town
C. London
D. New York City

100.      **What was the name of the American author who wrote 'The Electric Kool-Aid Acid Test', a book that became a key work of 1960s counterculture?**
A. Hunter S. Thompson
B. Jack Kerouac
C. Ken Kesey
D. Tom Wolfe

# Memories from the 1960s

*Your stories and experiences from the 1960s:*

# The 1960s Word Search Challenge

```
M  S  M  Z  O  L  W  X  C  U  N  M  T  V  F
S  E  L  N  X  N  U  K  X  N  I  Z  V  Q  X
I  I  K  P  G  N  I  D  N  A  L  N  O  O  M
N  P  U  K  Y  N  M  K  E  N  N  E  D  Y  F
I  P  C  M  M  A  W  Y  P  S  G  P  N  S  L
M  I  Q  I  N  E  B  O  I  E  S  C  S  O  O
E  H  K  T  V  E  K  S  T  Y  A  B  A  V  W
F  B  E  X  A  I  I  C  C  O  L  C  N  K  E
Y  I  K  T  B  R  L  H  O  C  M  G  E  O  R
V  A  L  O  C  G  E  R  B  T  F  M  G  R  P
H  E  S  A  Y  D  D  Q  I  B  S  D  L  X  O
S  M  B  F  E  M  Z  C  H  G  X  D  C  G  W
Z  U  O  L  O  L  L  O  P  A  H  X  O  L  E
C  M  I  N  I  S  K  I  R  T  B  T  Q  O  R
E  C  A  R  E  C  A  P  S  Y  I  V  S  P  W
```

| Apollo | Peace | Kennedy | CivilRights |
| --- | --- | --- | --- |
| CubaCrisis | Vietnam | MoonLanding | FlowerPower |
| Hippies | Beatles | Psychedelic | Miniskirt |
| MLK | Feminism | Woodstock | Motown |

# Section 3: The 1970s

A Decade of Change and Innovation

Welcome to the 1970s – a decade characterized by remarkable change, social progress, and an explosion of new cultural phenomena. From the end of the Vietnam War to the rise of disco and the environmental movement, the 1970s were a time of both challenges and triumphs. In this section, we'll explore the pivotal moments and iconic figures that defined this unique era.

# 1970s Trivia Questions

1. **Which U.S. President resigned in 1974 following the Watergate scandal?**
   A. Richard Nixon
   B. Gerald Ford
   C. Jimmy Carter
   D. Lyndon B. Johnson
2. **The 1970s saw the rise of a new music genre characterized by a steady four-on-the-floor beat and rich orchestration. What was this genre called?**
   A. Rock
   B. Punk
   C. Disco
   D. Hip Hop
3. **Which landmark U.S. Supreme Court decision in 1973 affirmed a woman's right to choose an abortion?**
   A. Brown v. Board of Education
   B. Roe v. Wade
   C. Miranda v. Arizona
   D. Loving v. Virginia
4. **In 1971, which country's civil war led to the creation of Bangladesh?**
   A. Pakistan
   B. India
   C. Nepal
   D. Myanmar

5. **What was the name of the space station launched by the Soviet Union in 1971, the first in space history?**
A. Mir
B. Sputnik
C. Skylab
D. Salyut 1

6. **Who was the revolutionary leader of the Khmer Rouge in Cambodia, responsible for one of the most brutal genocides of the 20th century?**
A. Pol Pot
B. Mao Zedong
C. Ho Chi Minh
D. Kim Il-sung

7. **Which 1975 film, directed by Steven Spielberg, is often credited with creating the summer blockbuster?**
A. Star Wars
B. The Exorcist
C. Jaws
D. The Godfather

8. **The Vietnam War ended in 1975 with the fall of Saigon to North Vietnamese forces. What is Saigon now known as?**
A. Hanoi
B. Ho Chi Minh City
C. Phnom Penh
D. Bangkok

9. **What was the major environmental event in 1970 that gave rise to annual global observances for environmental protection?**
A. The establishment of the EPA
B. The passing of the Clean Air Act
C. The first Earth Day
D. The Cuyahoga River fire

10. **Which iconic rock band released their influential album "The Dark Side of the Moon" in 1973?**
A. The Beatles
B. Led Zeppelin
C. Pink Floyd
D. The Rolling Stones

11. **Who became the first female Prime Minister of the United Kingdom in 1979?**
A. Margaret Thatcher
B. Indira Gandhi
C. Golda Meir
D. Elizabeth II

12. **The 1972 Olympic Games in Munich were overshadowed by a tragic event involving the kidnapping and murder of athletes from which country?**
A. United States
B. Soviet Union
C. Israel
D. Germany

13.     What was the popular dance move associated with disco music that became a craze in the late 1970s?
A. The Moonwalk
B. The Hustle
C. The Twist
D. The Macarena

14.     In 1979, a major nuclear accident occurred at Three Mile Island in which U.S. state?
A. New York
B. Pennsylvania
C. California
D. New Jersey

15.     Which treaty, signed in 1978 between Egypt and Israel, was a significant step towards Middle East peace?
A. Oslo Accords
B. Camp David Accords
C. Sykes-Picot Agreement
D. Treaty of Versailles

16.     The blockbuster movie 'Star Wars', a significant film in pop culture history, was released in which year?
A. 1977
B. 1978
C. 1979
D. 1980

17.     Which 1970s musical movement, characterized by its anti-establishment

ethos and DIY attitude, had bands like the Ramones and The Sex Pistols?
A. Disco
B. Funk
C. Punk Rock
D. New Wave

18. **Who was the charismatic leader behind the Jonestown Massacre, one of the largest mass suicides in history, in 1978?**
A. Charles Manson
B. Jim Jones
C. David Koresh
D. Marshall Applewhite

19. **In 1971, Intel released the 4004, an important early product in the development of what technology?**
A. Personal computers
B. Mobile phones
C. Microprocessors
D. Solar panels

20. **The Aswan High Dam, completed in 1970, is located in which country?**
A. Ethiopia
B. Egypt
C. Sudan
D. Libya

21. **Which American television series, first airing in 1971, became known for its edgy, socially conscious content and launched the career of Norman Lear?**

A. M*A*S*H
B. All in the Family
C. The Mary Tyler Moore Show
D. The Waltons

**22.    What major environmental disaster occurred in 1978, involving a supertanker named the Amoco Cadiz?**
A. A nuclear meltdown
B. An oil spill
C. A toxic gas leak
D. A forest fire

**23.    The first test tube baby, Louise Brown, was born in 1978 through in vitro fertilization in which country?**
A. United States
B. United Kingdom
C. Canada
D. Australia

**24.    Which American athlete won a record-breaking seven gold medals in swimming at the 1972 Munich Olympics?**
A. Mark Spitz
B. Michael Phelps
C. Greg Louganis
D. Matt Biondi

**25.    'Saturday Night Fever', a 1977 film that helped popularize disco music, starred which actor?**
A. Al Pacino
B. Robert De Niro

C. John Travolta

D. Dustin Hoffman

26.     **The 1970s oil crisis, which caused global economic and political turmoil, was primarily triggered by an embargo from which group of countries?**

A. OPEC

B. NATO

C. The European Union

D. The Warsaw Pact

27.     **What iconic video game, marking the start of the video gaming industry, was released by Atari in 1972?**

A. Space Invaders

B. Donkey Kong

C. Pac-Man

D. Pong

28.     **In 1974, Hank Aaron broke Babe Ruth's home run record in Major League Baseball. Which team was he playing for at the time?**

A. New York Yankees

B. Atlanta Braves

C. Chicago Cubs

D. Los Angeles Dodgers

29.     **Which revolutionary product, the first of its kind, was introduced by Sony in 1979, changing the way people listened to music?**

A. The iPod

B. The Walkman

C. The Boombox

D. The MP3 Player

30.      **The 1979 Iranian Revolution resulted in the overthrow of the Shah and the establishment of an Islamic Republic under which leader?**

A. Mahmoud Ahmadinejad

B. Ayatollah Ruhollah Khomeini

C. Mohammed Reza Pahlavi

D. Hassan Rouhani

31.      **The historic Apollo-Soyuz Test Project in 1975 marked the first international space mission conducted jointly by which two countries?**

A. United States and Soviet Union

B. United States and China

C. Soviet Union and France

D. United Kingdom and United States

32.      **In 1979, Mother Teresa was awarded the Nobel Peace Prize for her work with the poor in which city?**

A. Rome

B. Calcutta

C. New York

D. Nairobi

33.      **Which groundbreaking television miniseries, first aired in 1977, depicted the saga of an American family over several generations, starting with the Atlantic slave trade?**

A. Roots

B. The Thorn Birds

C. North and South

D. The Waltons

34.     **The Concorde, the first supersonic passenger airliner, began service in 1976. It was a joint project between which two countries?**

A. United States and Soviet Union

B. France and United Kingdom

C. Germany and Italy

D. Canada and United States

35.     **Who became the first woman to reach the top of Mount Everest in 1975?**

A. Tenzing Norgay

B. Reinhold Messner

C. Junko Tabei

D. Sir Edmund Hillary

36.     **In 1972, the video game 'Pong' was released, becoming one of the earliest arcade games. Which company created it?**

A. Nintendo

B. Sega

C. Atari

D. Sony

37.     **In 1976, Steve Jobs, Steve Wozniak, and Ronald Wayne founded which influential technology company?**

A. Microsoft

B. IBM

C. Apple

D. Google

38. **What was the major political scandal in 1972 that eventually led to the resignation of U.S. President Richard Nixon?**

A. Iran-Contra Affair

B. Watergate Scandal

C. Whitewater Controversy

D. Lewinsky Scandal

39. **In 1977, which country's military staged a coup led by General Zia-ul-Haq, overthrowing Prime Minister Zulfikar Ali Bhutto?**

A. Iran

B. India

C. Bangladesh

D. Pakistan

40. **Which American author published the influential feminist work 'The Female Eunuch' in 1970?**

A. Betty Friedan

B. Simone de Beauvoir

C. Germaine Greer

D. Gloria Steinem

41. **'Hotel California', a hit song and album by the Eagles, was released in which year?**

A. 1975

B. 1976

C. 1977

D. 1978

42. **In 1971, which amendment lowered the voting age in the United States from 21 to 18?**
A. 24th Amendment
B. 25th Amendment
C. 26th Amendment
D. 27th Amendment

43. **The term 'microprocessor' was first used in a paper published by which company in 1971?**
A. IBM
B. Intel
C. AMD
D. Texas Instruments

44. **Which iconic film directed by Francis Ford Coppola and starring Marlon Brando was released in 1972?**
A. Apocalypse Now
B. Taxi Driver
C. The Godfather
D. Raging Bull

45. **What landmark environmental law, passed in the United States in 1970, established the framework for modern environmental policy?**
A. The Clean Air Act
B. The Endangered Species Act
C. The National Environmental Policy Act
D. The Clean Water Act

46.     **Which American political scandal, resulting in the resignation of Vice President Spiro Agnew, took place in 1973?**
A. Watergate Scandal
B. Iran-Contra Affair
C. Whitewater Controversy
D. The Bribery Scandal

47.     **The iconic boxing match "The Rumble in the Jungle," featuring Muhammad Ali and George Foreman, took place in 1974 in which country?**
A. United States
B. Philippines
C. Zaire (now the Democratic Republic of the Congo)
D. South Africa

48.     **In 1970, which band released their final studio album, 'Let It Be'?**
A. The Rolling Stones
B. The Beatles
C. Pink Floyd
D. Led Zeppelin

49.     **Who was the first female Secretary of State in the United States, appointed by President Jimmy Carter in 1977?**
A. Madeleine Albright
B. Condoleezza Rice
C. Hillary Clinton
D. Patricia Roberts Harris

50. **The 1970s were marked by a significant movement in cinema known as 'New Hollywood.' Which of these films is considered a part of this movement?**
A. The Godfather
B. Gone with the Wind
C. Casablanca
D. Psycho

51. **Which country experienced a major revolution in 1979, resulting in the establishment of an Islamic Republic?**
A. Afghanistan
B. Pakistan
C. Iran
D. Iraq

52. **In 1973, the world experienced an oil crisis due to an embargo imposed by OPEC in response to U.S. support for Israel during which conflict?**
A. The Six-Day War
B. The Gulf War
C. The Yom Kippur War
D. The Iran-Iraq War

53. **The 1976 outbreak of which disease in Africa led to its naming after a nearby river?**
A. Ebola
B. Zika
C. Nile Virus
D. Marburg

54.     **Which treaty, signed in 1975, was a major step towards reducing Cold War tensions and promoting peace and cooperation in Europe?**
A. The Treaty of Rome
B. The Warsaw Pact
C. The Helsinki Accords
D. The NATO Treaty

55.     **Who directed the influential 1971 film 'A Clockwork Orange'?**
A. Alfred Hitchcock
B. Martin Scorsese
C. Francis Ford Coppola
D. Stanley Kubrick

56.     **The 1970s saw the emergence of environmental activism. In 1972, which international conference in Stockholm marked the first major global forum on environmental issues?**
A. The Earth Summit
B. The Kyoto Protocol
C. The United Nations Conference on the Human Environment
D. The Paris Agreement

57.     **In 1979, Margaret Thatcher became the first female Prime Minister of which country?**
A. United States
B. United Kingdom
C. Canada

D. Australia

58.    **The 1978 Camp David Accords were a peace agreement between Israel and which other Middle Eastern country?**
A. Egypt
B. Jordan
C. Lebanon
D. Syria

59.    **Which groundbreaking science fiction film, released in 1977, began one of the most popular and influential franchises in movie history?**
A. 2001: A Space Odyssey
B. Star Wars: A New Hope
C. Close Encounters of the Third Kind
D. Blade Runner

60.    **The 1972 Winter Olympics, marked by memorable performances and Cold War tensions, were held in which Japanese city?**
A. Tokyo
B. Nagano
C. Sapporo
D. Osaka

61.    **Which groundbreaking legislation, passed in the United States in 1972, prohibited gender discrimination in federally funded education programs?**
A. Title IX
B. Title VII
C. The Equal Rights Amendment

D. The Civil Rights Act

62. **In 1979, the Sony Walkman revolutionized personal music listening. In which country was the Sony Walkman developed?**

A. United States

B. Germany

C. Japan

D. South Korea

63. **Which controversial policy, aimed at controlling population growth, was introduced in China in 1979?**

A. One-Family-One-Child Policy

B. Two-Child Policy

C. One-Child Policy

D. Family Planning Policy

64. **In 1975, Microsoft was founded by Bill Gates and which other co-founder?**

A. Paul Allen

B. Steve Jobs

C. Steve Wozniak

D. Larry Ellison

65. **The 1970s saw the end of the Bretton Woods system and the beginning of freely floating exchange rates. In which year did this shift occur?**

A. 1971

B. 1973

C. 1975

D. 1977

66.    **Who was the Egyptian President who played a pivotal role in negotiating the Camp David Accords of 1978?**
A. Gamal Abdel Nasser
B. Anwar Sadat
C. Hosni Mubarak
D. Mohamed Morsi

67.    **In 1974, Hank Aaron broke Babe Ruth's long-standing home run record. Which Major League Baseball team did he play for at that time?**
A. Milwaukee Brewers
B. Atlanta Braves
C. Los Angeles Dodgers
D. New York Yankees

68.    **The 1970s saw the rise of environmental awareness. In 1970, which day was first celebrated as a day to focus on the environment?**
A. Earth Day
B. Green Day
C. Nature Day
D. World Environment Day

69.    **In 1974, which country experienced a revolution that ended decades of dictatorship and led to it becoming a democracy?**
A. Portugal
B. Spain
C. Greece

D. Brazil

70.     **'ABBA', a pop group that gained immense worldwide popularity, won the Eurovision Song Contest in 1974 with which song?**
A. "Dancing Queen"
B. "Mamma Mia"
C. "Waterloo"
D. "Fernando"

71.     **Which landmark U.S. Supreme Court case in 1978 upheld affirmative action, but with some limitations?**
A. Plessy v. Ferguson
B. Brown v. Board of Education
C. Regents of the University of California v. Bakke
D. Roe v. Wade

72.     **The first episode of 'Saturday Night Live', a show that would become a television institution, aired in which year?**
A. 1972
B. 1975
C. 1977
D. 1980

73.     **In 1971, which organization was founded by a group of activists in Vancouver, aiming to promote peace and environmental protection?**
A. Amnesty International
B. World Wildlife Fund

C. Greenpeace

D. Oxfam

74.     **Which infamous serial killer, who committed his crimes in the 1970s, was finally apprehended in 1975?**

A. Ted Bundy

B. John Wayne Gacy

C. Richard Ramirez

D. Jeffrey Dahmer

75.     **The 1972 Summer Olympics, held in Munich, Germany, were tragically marred by an act of terrorism against athletes from which country?**

A. United States

B. Israel

C. Russia

D. Germany

76.     **What was the name of the first video game console released by Atari in 1977, popularizing home video gaming?**

A. Magnavox Odyssey

B. Nintendo Entertainment System

C. Atari 2600

D. ColecoVision

77.     **In 1976, which African country achieved independence from Portugal, following a protracted liberation war?**

A. Mozambique

B. Angola

C. Guinea-Bissau

D. Cape Verde

78. **Who was the first woman appointed to the United States Supreme Court, nominated by President Jimmy Carter in 1979?**
A. Ruth Bader Ginsburg
B. Sandra Day O'Connor
C. Sonia Sotomayor
D. None; the first woman was appointed in the 1980s

79. **The 1973 Arab-Israeli war is also known by what name, referring to the Jewish holiday during which it began?**
A. The Passover War
B. The Hanukkah War
C. The Yom Kippur War
D. The Rosh Hashanah War

80. **Which British band released the concept album 'The Wall' in 1979, one of the best-selling albums of all time?**
A. The Beatles
B. Led Zeppelin
C. Pink Floyd
D. The Rolling Stones

81. **What major event in 1979 marked the beginning of the end of the Cold War, involving a significant shift in U.S.-Soviet relations?**
A. The Helsinki Accords
B. The Soviet invasion of Afghanistan

C. The Salt II Treaty
D. The Reykjavik Summit

82.    **'Grease', a popular musical film starring John Travolta and Olivia Newton-John, was released in which year?**
A. 1975
B. 1977
C. 1978
D. 1980

83.    **In 1973, the American Psychiatric Association made a landmark decision regarding the classification of homosexuality. What was the decision?**
A. Classified as a mental illness
B. Declassified as a mental illness
C. Recognized as a genetic trait
D. No change in classification

84.    **The 1970s saw a revolution in computer technology. Which company introduced the first commercially successful microcomputer in 1977?**
A. IBM
B. Microsoft
C. Apple
D. Tandy Corporation / RadioShack

85.    **Which major automotive company introduced the first Japanese luxury car, the Lexus, at the end of the 1970s?**
A. Toyota
B. Nissan

C. Honda

D. Subaru

86.     **In 1974, India conducted its first nuclear test, joining the ranks of nuclear-armed nations. What was the test codenamed?**

A. Operation Shakti

B. Smiling Buddha

C. Pokhran-I

D. Thunderbolt

87.     **Which landmark U.S. legislation, passed in 1972, was designed to protect endangered species and their habitats?**

A. The Clean Air Act

B. The Endangered Species Act

C. The Clean Water Act

D. The National Environmental Policy Act

88.     **The 1970s saw the rise of personal computing. Who is credited with inventing the personal computer in 1973?**

A. Steve Jobs

B. Bill Gates

C. Alan Turing

D. Xerox PARC researchers

89.     **In 1979, which Caribbean country experienced a revolution that resulted in a shift towards socialism and alignment with the Soviet Union?**

A. Jamaica

B. Cuba

C. Grenada

D. Dominican Republic

90. **Who was the famous American singer and actor who passed away in 1977, becoming a cultural icon of the 20th century?**

A. Frank Sinatra

B. Elvis Presley

C. John Lennon

D. Jim Morrison

91. **What significant event in the world of chess took place in 1972, involving American chess player Bobby Fischer?**

A. He won the World Chess Championship

B. He invented a new style of chess

C. He retired from professional chess

D. He lost the championship in a historic match

92. **In 1977, the U.S. launched the Voyager 1 spacecraft. What was its primary mission?**

A. To land on Mars

B. To study Jupiter and Saturn

C. To exit the Solar System

D. To orbit the Earth

93. **The Torrijos–Carter Treaties, transferring control of the Panama Canal, were signed in 1977 between Panama and which other country?**

A. United States

B. United Kingdom

C. Spain

D. France

94. **Which iconic horror film, directed by Ridley Scott, was released in 1979 and became renowned for its atmospheric tension and design?**
A. The Shining
B. The Exorcist
C. Alien
D. Halloween

95. **The first Gay Pride marches in the United States were held in 1970 to commemorate the first anniversary of what event?**
A. The Stonewall Riots
B. The first same-sex marriage
C. The decriminalization of homosexuality
D. The founding of the LGBT movement

96. **In 1970, who became the first female Prime Minister of Israel?**
A. Golda Meir
B. Margaret Thatcher
C. Indira Gandhi
D. Benazir Bhutto

97. **What was the name of the famous agreement signed in 1975 that laid the groundwork for peaceful relations and cooperation in post-World War II Europe?**
A. The Treaty of Rome
B. The Warsaw Pact
C. The Helsinki Accords

D. The NATO Treaty

98.     **In 1975, which Southeast Asian country was taken over by the Communist Pathet Lao, marking the end of a long civil war?**
A. Vietnam
B. Cambodia
C. Laos
D. Thailand

99.     **Which influential 1970s TV series, created by Norman Lear, was known for its depiction of a working-class American family and tackled numerous social issues?**
A. MAS*H
B. All in the Family
C. The Mary Tyler Moore Show
D. Sanford and Son

100.     **The 1973 oil crisis, which led to worldwide economic turmoil, was primarily caused by an embargo imposed by OPEC in response to Western support for Israel during which conflict?**
A. The Six-Day War
B. The Gulf War
C. The Yom Kippur War
D. The Iran-Iraq War

# Memories from the 1970s

*Your stories and experiences from the 1970s:*

# The 1970s Word Search Challenge

```
N  I  X  O  N  D  D  O  J  P  Y  Q  E  V  S
M  D  S  R  P  Q  W  C  F  T  P  T  K  I  B
S  O  Z  R  B  J  B  S  M  R  A  Q  S  E  I
I  B  I  M  A  A  I  I  L  G  K  I  L  T  R
N  A  I  D  L  W  C  D  R  R  R  L  P  N  A
I  H  P  Y  U  R  R  E  G  C  B  C  S  A  T
M  C  K  O  O  T  T  A  L  O  R  O  Z  M  A
E  S  N  S  L  A  S  I  T  L  P  N  I  W  S
F  C  O  X  W  L  O  T  S  S  U  C  H  A  B
U  F  W  V  H  L  O  X  V  J  P  O  M  R  Q
T  J  A  W  S  M  I  E  X  Z  S  R  O  E  T
G  Y  W  W  S  P  X  W  U  M  Y  D  E  N  X
K  C  O  R  K  N  U  P  L  X  F  E  U  D  S
P  U  K  A  E  R  B  S  E  L  T  A  E  B  N
E  L  V  I  S  P  R  E  S  L  E  Y  E  M  I
```

| BellBottoms | Studio | Nixon | OilCrisis |
| --- | --- | --- | --- |
| ElvisPresley | Atari | Skylab | StarWars |
| Microsoft | Concorde | Disco | Watergate |
| PunkRock | Feminism | Jaws | Beatles |

# Section 4: The 1980s

A Decade of Transformation and Innovation

Welcome to the 1980s – a decade marked by dramatic political shifts, rapid technological progress, and distinctive cultural expressions. From the fall of the Berlin Wall to the rise of digital technology and the explosion of pop culture, the 1980s were a time of significant change and memorable moments. In this section, we'll delve into the key events and iconic figures that defined this vibrant era.

# 1980s Trivia Questions

1. **Which event, occurring in 1989, symbolized the end of the Cold War?**
   A. The signing of the INF Treaty
   B. The dissolution of the Soviet Union
   C. The fall of the Berlin Wall
   D. The end of the Vietnam War

2. **In the realm of technology, the 1980s saw the introduction of the first commercially successful personal computer by IBM. What year was it launched?**
   A. 1981
   B. 1983
   C. 1985
   D. 1987

3. **Which music television channel, launching in 1981, had a profound impact on the music industry and popular culture?**
   A. VH1
   B. MTV
   C. BET
   D. CMT

4. **Who was the first woman appointed to the United States Supreme Court, nominated by President Ronald Reagan in 1981?**
   A. Ruth Bader Ginsburg
   B. Sandra Day O'Connor
   C. Sonia Sotomayor
   D. Elena Kagan

5. In 1984, which territory was handed back to China by the United Kingdom under the terms of the Sino-British Joint Declaration?
A. Hong Kong
B. Macau
C. Singapore
D. Shanghai

6. What was the name of the space shuttle that tragically exploded shortly after liftoff in 1986, leading to a pause in the Space Shuttle program?
A. Challenger
B. Columbia
C. Discovery
D. Atlantis

7. Which disease was identified in the early 1980s, leading to a major global health crisis?
A. SARS
B. HIV/AIDS
C. Ebola
D. H1N1 Influenza

8. The 1980s video game revolution was marked by the release of which iconic arcade game in 1980?
A. Space Invaders
B. Donkey Kong
C. Pac-Man
D. Tetris

9. **In 1986, the United States and the Soviet Union agreed to eliminate intermediate-range nuclear weapons in a treaty known as what?**
A. The START Treaty
B. The SALT Treaty
C. The INF Treaty
D. The ABM Treaty

10. **The anti-apartheid movement gained international attention in the 1980s, particularly through the activism of which South African leader?**
A. Desmond Tutu
B. Nelson Mandela
C. Oliver Tambo
D. Thabo Mbeki

11. **Which famous environmental disaster, known as the worst nuclear accident in history, occurred in 1986?**
A. The Three Mile Island accident
B. The Fukushima Daiichi nuclear disaster
C. The Chernobyl disaster
D. The Bhopal disaster

12. **Who was elected as the President of the Philippines in 1986, restoring democracy after the fall of Ferdinand Marcos?**
A. Gloria Macapagal Arroyo
B. Benigno Aquino III
C. Corazon Aquino
D. Rodrigo Duterte

13.    **Which iconic concert held in 1985 was organized to raise funds for famine relief in Ethiopia?**
A. Woodstock
B. Live Aid
C. The Concert for Bangladesh
D. Farm Aid

14.    **In 1982, the United Kingdom and Argentina went to war over which territory?**
A. The Falkland Islands
B. Gibraltar
C. South Georgia Island
D. The Canary Islands

15.    **Which famous American artist, known for his pop art and paintings of Campbell's soup cans, died in 1987?**
A. Roy Lichtenstein
B. Jackson Pollock
C. Andy Warhol
D. Jean-Michel Basquiat

16.    **The iconic video game character Mario, who became a symbol of Nintendo, made his debut in which 1981 arcade game?**
A. Super Mario Bros.
B. Mario Kart
C. Donkey Kong
D. The Legend of Zelda

17.    **In 1983, President Ronald Reagan announced the Strategic Defense Initiative, also known colloquially as what?**

A. Star Wars
B. Space Force
C. Sky Shield
D. Starfleet Command

18. **Which influential 1980s TV show, featuring glamorous women and complex business dealings, centered around the oil industry in Texas?**
A. Dallas
B. Dynasty
C. Falcon Crest
D. Knots Landing

19. **The 1980s saw the rise of the personal computer. Which company released the Macintosh, a significant early personal computer, in 1984?**
A. IBM
B. Microsoft
C. Apple
D. Hewlett-Packard

20. **In 1985, Mikhail Gorbachev became the leader of the Soviet Union and began policies of glasnost and perestroika. What was the primary goal of these policies?**
A. To expand the Soviet Union's military power
B. To maintain the traditional Soviet communist ideology
C. To open up the Soviet society and economy
D. To strengthen the Soviet Union's control over Eastern Europe

21.     What was the name of the NASA space probe that became the first to visit Saturn, providing detailed images and data about the planet and its moons in 1980?
A. Voyager 1
B. Voyager 2
C. Galileo
D. Cassini

22.     In 1984, the United Kingdom and China signed the Sino-British Joint Declaration, agreeing to return which territory to China in 1997?
A. Hong Kong
B. Macau
C. Singapore
D. Shanghai

23.     Which popular diet soda was introduced by the Coca-Cola Company in 1982?
A. Diet Coke
B. Coke Zero
C. Pepsi Max
D. Diet Pepsi

24.     In the 1980s, this music duo became widely popular for their unique sound and image, including hits like "West End Girls" and "It's a Sin." Who are they?
A. Erasure
B. Wham!
C. Pet Shop Boys

D. Tears for Fears

25. **The Iran-Contra affair, a political scandal in the United States, involved secretly selling arms to Iran and diverting the proceeds to support rebels in which country?**
A. Afghanistan
B. Nicaragua
C. Cuba
D. El Salvador

26. **Which American musician released the best-selling album of the 1980s, "Thriller," in 1982?**
A. Prince
B. Madonna
C. Michael Jackson
D. Bruce Springsteen

27. **In 1986, the United States observed the first federal holiday in honor of which civil rights leader?**
A. Malcolm X
B. Rosa Parks
C. Martin Luther King Jr.
D. Frederick Douglass

28. **Which science fiction film, released in 1982 and directed by Ridley Scott, became a cult classic and is known for its futuristic depiction of Los Angeles?**
A. Blade Runner
B. The Terminator

C. Alien

D. Star Trek II: The Wrath of Khan

29. **The anti-communist revolutions of 1989, leading to the fall of communist regimes in Central and Eastern Europe, began in which country?**

A. Poland

B. East Germany

C. Czechoslovakia

D. Romania

30. **Which groundbreaking personal computer, introduced by Apple in 1984, featured a graphical user interface and a mouse?**

A. Apple Lisa

B. Apple I

C. Apple II

D. Apple Macintosh

31. **In 1989, the Velvet Revolution peacefully overthrew communist rule in which European country?**

A. Poland

B. Hungary

C. Czechoslovakia

D. East Germany

32. **Which iconic 1980s movie, directed by John Hughes, features five high school students serving detention together?**

A. Ferris Bueller's Day Off

B. The Breakfast Club
C. Sixteen Candles
D. Pretty in Pink

**33.    In 1983, which compact disc (CD) was the first to be manufactured for commercial release?**
A. "The Visitors" by ABBA
B. "52nd Street" by Billy Joel
C. "Thriller" by Michael Jackson
D. "Born in the U.S.A." by Bruce Springsteen

**34.    The first case of what would later be known as AIDS was reported in 1981. Which group was initially, and mistakenly, believed to be primarily affected?**
A. Hemophiliacs
B. Intravenous drug users
C. Homosexual men
D. Heterosexual women

**35.    In 1984, the United Kingdom and China signed a joint declaration regarding the future of Hong Kong. When was Hong Kong officially handed back to China?**
A. 1987
B. 1992
C. 1997
D. 2001

**36.    Which famous video game, featuring falling block puzzles, was created by a Soviet software engineer in 1984?**
A. Super Mario Bros.

B. Pac-Man
C. Space Invaders
D. Tetris

37.     **In 1980, the United States boycotted the Summer Olympics held in Moscow due to what international event?**
A. The Vietnam War
B. The Soviet-Afghan War
C. The Iran Hostage Crisis
D. The Cold War

38.     **Which iconic British band, known for hits like "Under Pressure" and "Another One Bites the Dust," performed at Live Aid in 1985 and experienced a resurgence in popularity?**
A. The Beatles
B. The Rolling Stones
C. Pink Floyd
D. Queen

39.     **In 1981, Sandra Day O'Connor was appointed to the Supreme Court, making her the first woman to serve as a Justice. Who nominated her?**
A. Jimmy Carter
B. Ronald Reagan
C. George H.W. Bush
D. Richard Nixon

40.     **The tragic explosion of the Space Shuttle Challenger occurred how many seconds after liftoff in 1986?**

A. 73 seconds

B. 58 seconds

C. 89 seconds

D. 102 seconds

41.     **In 1985, Mikhail Gorbachev became the General Secretary of the Communist Party in the Soviet Union. What was his policy of openness and transparency known as?**

A. Perestroika

B. Glasnost

C. Detente

D. Realpolitik

42.     **Which popular 1980s TV series featured a time-traveling scientist and his young companion traveling in a DeLorean?**

A. Doctor Who

B. Quantum Leap

C. Back to the Future: The Animated Series

D. Star Trek: The Next Generation

43.     **In 1989, the Tiananmen Square protests in Beijing were primarily led by which group?**

A. Factory workers

B. University students

C. Peasants

D. Military dissidents

44.     **Which American artist, known for combining graffiti and fine art, gained**

widespread recognition in the 1980s before his untimely death in 1988?
A. Keith Haring
B. Andy Warhol
C. Jean-Michel Basquiat
D. Roy Lichtenstein

45. **In 1980, who became the first female Prime Minister of the United Kingdom?**
A. Margaret Thatcher
B. Indira Gandhi
C. Golda Meir
D. Angela Merkel

46. **The 1980s was a significant decade for video gaming. Which iconic platform game, featuring siblings trying to rescue a princess, was released by Nintendo in 1985?**
A. The Legend of Zelda
B. Donkey Kong
C. Super Mario Bros.
D. Metroid

47. **In 1980, the eruption of Mount St. Helens occurred in which U.S. state?**
A. California
B. Washington
C. Oregon
D. Alaska

48. **The hit 1985 film 'Back to the Future' was directed by whom?**
A. Steven Spielberg
B. George Lucas

C. Robert Zemeckis

D. James Cameron

49.    **Who won the Nobel Peace Prize in 1983 for his efforts to end Poland's communist dictatorship through the Solidarity movement?**

A. Mikhail Gorbachev

B. Lech Wałęsa

C. Vaclav Havel

D. Pope John Paul II

50.    **In 1983, which Korean Air Lines flight was shot down by Soviet fighters, heightening Cold War tensions?**

A. Flight 007

B. Flight 902

C. Flight 858

D. Flight 801

51.    **'Do They Know It's Christmas?', a charity single raising funds for famine relief in Ethiopia, was recorded in 1984 by a group known as what?**

A. USA for Africa

B. Band Aid

C. Live Aid

D. We Are the World

52.    **The anti-apartheid leader Nelson Mandela was imprisoned on Robben Island for most of the 1980s until his release in what year?**

A. 1980

B. 1988

C. 1990

D. 1992

53.    **Which famous American entrepreneur founded the cable television network CNN in 1980?**

A. Rupert Murdoch

B. Ted Turner

C. Sumner Redstone

D. John Malone

54.    **In 1986, a nuclear reactor at the Chernobyl Nuclear Power Plant in the Soviet Union exploded, resulting in one of the worst nuclear disasters in history. Where is Chernobyl located?**

A. Ukraine

B. Russia

C. Belarus

D. Kazakhstan

55.    **What was the best-selling video game console of the 1980s, introduced by Nintendo in 1985?**

A. Atari 2600

B. Sega Genesis

C. Nintendo Entertainment System (NES)

D. Game Boy

56.    **In 1981, the first Space Shuttle, named Columbia, was launched by NASA. What was significant about this spacecraft?**

A. It was the first to land on the Moon

B. It was the first reusable spacecraft
C. It was the first to use solar power
D. It was the first to carry a satellite

57.     **'E.T. the Extra-Terrestrial', a film that became a cultural phenomenon, was directed by which filmmaker in 1982?**
A. George Lucas
B. Steven Spielberg
C. Ridley Scott
D. James Cameron

58.     **The 1987 treaty known as the INF Treaty aimed to eliminate intermediate-range and shorter-range missiles. What does INF stand for?**
A. International Nuclear Forces
B. Intercontinental Nuclear Federation
C. Intermediate-Range Nuclear Forces
D. Integrated National Front

59.     **Which iconic 1980s TV series, featuring a wealthy and feuding family in the oil business, was a major hit?**
A. Dallas
B. Dynasty
C. Falcon Crest
D. The Colbys

60.     **In 1987, President Ronald Reagan famously challenged the Soviet Union's leader with the phrase "Tear down this wall!" referring to what?**
A. The Berlin Wall

B. The Iron Curtain

C. The Bamboo Curtain

D. The Great Firewall

61.    **In 1988, which catastrophic event led to the deaths of thousands of people in the city of Bhopal, India?**

A. A devastating earthquake

B. A severe flood

C. A chemical plant disaster

D. A major train collision

62.    **The popular fitness trend of aerobics, often associated with colorful attire and energetic music, became widespread during which decade?**

A. 1960s

B. 1970s

C. 1980s

D. 1990s

63.    **In 1985, which agreement was signed between the United States and Canada to address acid rain and air quality issues?**

A. The Great Lakes Accord

B. The Air Quality Agreement

C. The Clean Air Act

D. The Environmental Protection Treaty

64.    **The 1980s saw a surge in popularity for skateboarding. Which skateboarder, known for his vertical ramp prowess, became a household name during this time?**

A. Tony Hawk

B. Rodney Mullen

C. Steve Caballero

D. Danny Way

65.    **In 1989, the World Wide Web was invented by Tim Berners-Lee while working at which organization?**

A. NASA

B. Microsoft

C. CERN

D. IBM

66.    **In 1980, who was elected as the first female Prime Minister of Norway?**

A. Margaret Thatcher

B. Gro Harlem Brundtland

C. Vigdís Finnbogadóttir

D. Angela Merkel

67.    **The 1980s was marked by the popularity of video rental stores. Which movie rental company, founded in 1985, became synonymous with home movie and video game rentals?**

A. Netflix

B. Blockbuster

C. Redbox

D. Hollywood Video

68.    **'Thriller', released in 1982 by Michael Jackson, featured a groundbreaking music video directed by which filmmaker?**

A. George Lucas

B. Steven Spielberg

C. John Landis
D. Martin Scorsese

69.     **In 1989, the first GPS satellite was launched, paving the way for global navigation systems. What does GPS stand for?**
A. Global Positioning System
B. Geographical Placement Service
C. Global Pathway Satellite
D. Geospatial Pinging System

70.     **Who became the first African American woman to travel in space in 1983?**
A. Mae Jemison
B. Sally Ride
C. Kathryn Sullivan
D. Guion Bluford

71.     **In the 1980s, which British band became known for their innovative music videos and hits like "Hungry Like the Wolf" and "Rio"?**
A. The Cure
B. The Smiths
C. Duran Duran
D. Depeche Mode

72.     **Which 1982 science fiction film, directed by Ridley Scott and starring Harrison Ford, was based on Philip K. Dick's novel 'Do Androids Dream of Electric Sheep'?**
A. Blade Runner

B. The Terminator
C. Total Recall
D. A Scanner Darkly

73.    **In 1983, a Korean commercial airliner (KAL 007) was shot down after entering Soviet airspace, escalating tensions during the Cold War. What happened to the passengers and crew?**
A. They were all safely rescued.
B. They were detained in the Soviet Union.
C. They were all killed
D. They were released after negotiations.

74.    **Which iconic American music artist, known for hits like "Purple Rain" and "When Doves Cry," rose to fame in the 1980s?**
A. Michael Jackson
B. Madonna
C. Prince
D. Bruce Springsteen

75.    **The Chernobyl disaster in 1986 resulted in large areas being contaminated with radioactive material. This disaster occurred in which part of the Soviet Union?**
A. Russia
B. Ukraine
C. Belarus
D. Kazakhstan

76.    **The Iran-Iraq War, a prolonged military conflict between neighboring**

Middle Eastern countries, started in 1980 and lasted until which year?
A. 1984
B. 1986
C. 1988
D. 1990

77.     In 1984, which iconic Apple computer advertisement, directed by Ridley Scott, was aired during the Super Bowl?
A. The Lemmings ad
B. The "Think Different" ad
C. The "1984" ad
D. The "Hello" ad

78.     "Live Aid," a dual-venue concert in 1985, was organized by Bob Geldof and Midge Ure to raise funds for famine relief in which continent?
A. Asia
B. Africa
C. South America
D. Europe

79.     In 1983, Sally Ride became the first American woman in space aboard which Space Shuttle?
A. Challenger
B. Discovery
C. Atlantis
D. Columbia

80.     Which 1980s film, directed by John Hughes, stars Matthew Broderick as a high

school student who skips school for a day in Chicago?
A. Sixteen Candles
B. The Breakfast Club
C. Ferris Bueller's Day Off
D. Pretty in Pink

81.     The anti-establishment youth culture and music movement known as "punk" saw a resurgence in the 1980s, particularly in which country?
A. United States
B. United Kingdom
C. Germany
D. Australia

82.     The Microsoft Windows operating system was first introduced in which year of the 1980s?
A. 1980
B. 1983
C. 1985
D. 1988

83.     In 1987, who became the first man to fly solo non-stop around the world without refueling?
A. Charles Lindbergh
B. Steve Fossett
C. Richard Branson
D. Dick Rutan

84.     The "Just Say No" campaign, part of the war on drugs, was popularized in the

1980s by which First Lady of the United States?
A. Nancy Reagan
B. Betty Ford
C. Barbara Bush
D. Rosalynn Carter

85. In 1989, protests for democratic reform in Tiananmen Square in Beijing were met with military force. Which iconic image emerged from this event?
A. The Falling Man
B. The Tank Man
C. The Unknown Rebel
D. The Flag Raiser

86. The American space shuttle Discovery launched the Hubble Space Telescope into orbit in 1990, marking a significant advancement in astronomy. Who was the telescope named after?
A. Edwin Hubble
B. Carl Sagan
C. Isaac Newton
D. Galileo Galilei

87. Which action movie released in 1988, starring Bruce Willis as John McClane, became an iconic Christmas film for many?
A. Lethal Weapon
B. Die Hard
C. The Terminator
D. Rambo

88.     **In 1980, the United States led a boycott of the Summer Olympics held in Moscow in protest of what?**
A. The Soviet invasion of Afghanistan
B. The Cold War
C. Human rights violations
D. Nuclear arms race

89.     **The best-selling video game console of the 1980s was introduced by Nintendo. What was it called?**
A. Nintendo Entertainment System (NES)
B. Game Boy
C. Super Nintendo
D. Atari 2600

90.     **Which significant agreement, signed in 1987, aimed to protect the ozone layer by phasing out the production of numerous substances responsible for ozone depletion?**
A. The Kyoto Protocol
B. The Paris Agreement
C. The Montreal Protocol
D. The Copenhagen Accord

91.     **In 1985, Mikhail Gorbachev became the leader of the Soviet Union and introduced significant reforms. What was the policy of restructuring the economy called?**
A. Glasnost
B. Perestroika
C. Detente

D. Realpolitik

92.      **The iconic concert event 'Live Aid' in 1985 featured performances from various artists at stadiums in London and which other city?**
A. New York
B. Philadelphia
C. Los Angeles
D. Paris

93.      **The first cases of what would later be known as AIDS were reported in the early 1980s. What does AIDS stand for?**
A. Advanced Immune Deficiency Syndrome
B. Acquired Immune Deficiency Syndrome
C. Auto Immune Deficiency Syndrome
D. Acute Immuno Disorder Syndrome

94.      **The Rubik's Cube, a popular puzzle toy, became a global craze in the early 1980s. In which country was it invented?**
A. United States
B. Germany
C. Hungary
D. Japan

95.      **In 1981, the American hostages held in Iran were released after 444 days in captivity. Their release coincided with the inauguration of which U.S. President?**
A. Jimmy Carter
B. Ronald Reagan
C. George H. W. Bush

D. Richard Nixon

96.	'The Simpsons', one of the longest-running TV shows in history, first appeared as shorts on 'The Tracey Ullman Show' in what year?
A. 1985
B. 1987
C. 1989
D. 1991

97.	In 1983, President Ronald Reagan announced the Strategic Defense Initiative, a proposed missile defense system that was nicknamed what?
A. Star Wars
B. Sky Shield
C. Space Force
D. Orion Project

98.	'Pac-Man', one of the most popular video games of the 1980s, was originally released by Namco in which year?
A. 1980
B. 1982
C. 1984
D. 1986

99.	The fall of the Berlin Wall in 1989 was a significant event in the decline of communism in Eastern Europe. Which German city was reunified following this event?
A. Berlin

B. Munich

C. Frankfurt

D. Hamburg

100.    **In 1980, John Lennon, was tragically assassinated in which city?**

A. London

B. New York City

C. Los Angeles

D. San Francisco

# Memories from the 1980s

*Your stories and experiences from the 1980s:*

# The 1980s Word Search Challenge

```
M  D  W  J  B  A  B  T  M  J  P  V  V  J  V
K  E  H  A  V  F  A  L  K  L  A  N  D  S  A
C  H  A  L  L  E  N  G  E  R  C  H  Y  I  N
O  Y  K  V  R  N  H  G  A  L  M  M  D  A  M
R  V  S  T  P  U  B  C  L  N  A  S  M  X  P
M  F  O  M  S  N  B  A  A  C  N  K  O  G  U
A  T  Z  P  E  D  W  I  I  B  L  O  X  W  K
L  B  D  R  R  N  W  N  K  A  R  Y  D  M  S
G  A  E  C  I  A  T  P  W  C  F  O  K  A  C
O  O  N  L  P  O  H  P  I  H  U  Q  G  P  M
E  I  R  A  S  Y  E  H  F  I  U  B  M  T  G
Y  E  R  H  G  L  L  Y  B  O  N  R  E  H  C
B  F  O  Q  A  A  N  I  N  T  E  N  D  O  U
X  V  X  F  P  P  E  D  B  G  R  Q  B  L  N
X  N  U  C  K  E  U  R  Y  E  H  N  P  Y  G
```

| AIDS | Oprah | HipHop | Challenger |
|------|-------|--------|------------|
| Chernobyl | RubikCube | MTV | Macintosh |
| Gorbachev | BerlinWall | PacMan | Nintendo |
| Madonna | Falklands | Walkman | Reagan |

# Section 5: The 1990s

A Decade of Globalization and Technological Revolution

Welcome to the 1990s — a decade characterized by the rapid expansion of the internet, significant political realignments, and iconic pop culture moments. From the rise of the World Wide Web to the end of the Cold War, the 1990s were marked by rapid changes and advancements that shaped the modern world. In this section, we'll explore the memorable events, cultural milestones, and influential personalities that defined this era.

# 1990s Trivia Questions

1. **In 1991, the World Wide Web was launched to the public. Who is credited with inventing the World Wide Web?**
   A. Bill Gates
   B. Steve Jobs
   C. Tim Berners-Lee
   D. Mark Zuckerberg

2. **The dissolution of the Soviet Union, marking the end of the Cold War, occurred in which year?**
   A. 1989
   B. 1990
   C. 1991
   D. 1992

3. **Which popular gaming console, released by Sony in 1994, revolutionized 3D gaming?**
   A. Nintendo 64
   B. Sega Genesis
   C. Sony PlayStation
   D. Xbox

4. **The 1990s saw the rise of grunge music, primarily associated with which American city?**
   A. Los Angeles
   B. New York
   C. Seattle
   D. San Francisco

5. **In 1997, the world mourned the death of Princess Diana, who died in a car crash in which city?**
   A. London
   B. Paris
   C. Rome
   D. Madrid

6. **The iconic 1990s sitcom "Friends" first aired in what year?**
   A. 1992
   B. 1994
   C. 1996
   D. 1998

7. **Nelson Mandela was elected President of South Africa in 1994, marking the end of apartheid. What political party did he represent?**
   A. African National Congress
   B. Democratic Alliance
   C. Pan Africanist Congress
   D. National Party

8. **The Hubble Space Telescope, launched in 1990, was named after which American astronomer?**
   A. Carl Sagan
   B. Edwin Hubble
   C. Neil deGrasse Tyson
   D. Richard Feynman

9. **In 1995, a federal building in Oklahoma City was bombed, resulting in a tragic loss of life. Who was the main perpetrator of this attack?**
A. Timothy McVeigh
B. Ted Kaczynski
C. Ramzi Yousef
D. Eric Rudolph

10. **The Euro, a new currency for many European countries, was officially introduced in which year?**
A. 1992
B. 1995
C. 1999
D. 2002

11. **The popular book series "Harry Potter," written by J.K. Rowling, was first published in which year?**
A. 1995
B. 1997
C. 1999
D. 2001

12. **In 1996, a cloned sheep named Dolly was announced to the world, marking a significant scientific breakthrough. Where did this occur?**
A. United States
B. United Kingdom
C. Australia
D. Switzerland

13.     The 1990s was known for the "Dot-com Bubble," a period of massive growth in internet-based companies. In which year did this bubble reach its peak?
A. 1996
B. 1999
C. 2001
D. 2003

14.     In 1998, Google Inc. was founded by Larry Page and Sergey Brin while they were students at which university?
A. Harvard University
B. Massachusetts Institute of Technology
C. Stanford University
D. University of California, Berkeley

15.     "The Matrix," a groundbreaking science fiction film known for its visual effects, was released in which year?
A. 1997
B. 1998
C. 1999
D. 2000

16.     The 1994 FIFA World Cup, one of the most watched sporting events in the 1990s, was hosted by which country?
A. Brazil
B. Italy
C. United States
D. France

17.  **In 1992, the Maastricht Treaty was signed, leading to the creation of what?**
A. The United Nations
B. The European Union
C. NATO
D. The Commonwealth of Nations

18.  **Which technology company released Windows 95, a major advancement in personal computing, in 1995?**
A. Apple
B. IBM
C. Microsoft
D. Google

19.  **The Bosnian War, a major conflict in the Balkans following the breakup of Yugoslavia, lasted from 1992 until which year?**
A. 1995
B. 1996
C. 1997
D. 1998

20.  **In 1997, the British colony of Hong Kong was returned to which country?**
A. Japan
B. United Kingdom
C. United States
D. China

21.  **"Schindler's List," a film about the Holocaust directed by Steven Spielberg,**

won the Academy Award for Best Picture in which year?

A. 1993

B. 1994

C. 1995

D. 1996

22.　　In 1995, a historic peace agreement was signed in Northern Ireland, known as what?

A. The Belfast Agreement

B. The Easter Agreement

C. The Good Friday Agreement

D. The Dublin Accord

23.　　The Rwandan Genocide, a tragic conflict resulting in the deaths of hundreds of thousands, occurred in which year?

A. 1990

B. 1992

C. 1994

D. 1996

24.　　In 1998, which two tech giants merged in what was then the largest merger in history?

A. Microsoft and Apple

B. Google and Yahoo

C. AOL and Time Warner

D. IBM and Sun Microsystems

25.　　The first version of Java programming language was officially launched in which year, becoming a cornerstone of modern software development?

A. 1991

B. 1993

C. 1995

D. 1997

26. In 1990, Nelson Mandela was released from prison after 27 years. He was incarcerated for his role in fighting against what in South Africa?

A. Apartheid

B. Colonialism

C. Corruption

D. Communism

27. The popular TV show "Seinfeld" aired its final episode in which year, marking the end of one of the most successful sitcoms in television history?

A. 1996

B. 1998

C. 2000

D. 2002

28. In 1993, the European Single Market was completed, allowing for the free movement of goods, capital, services, and people among how many European countries?

A. 12

B. 15

C. 25

D. 27

29. **Who was elected as President of Russia in 1991, marking the end of the Soviet era?**
A. Mikhail Gorbachev
B. Vladimir Putin
C. Boris Yeltsin
D. Dmitry Medvedev

30. **The Oklahoma City Bombing, one of the deadliest acts of domestic terrorism in U.S. history, occurred in which year?**
A. 1993
B. 1995
C. 1997
D. 1999

31. **In 1999, the Euro was introduced as the official currency in several European countries. Which of the following was not an initial member of the Eurozone?**
A. Germany
B. France
C. United Kingdom
D. Italy

32. **The 1990s saw the emergence of a new genre in music known as "Britpop." Which of these bands was a leading figure in the Britpop movement?**
A. Blur
B. U2
C. The Rolling Stones
D. The Beatles

33. **In 1990, the Hubble Space Telescope was launched into space. However, it initially faced a significant issue. What was the problem?**
A. A faulty mirror
B. Solar panel failure
C. Computer malfunction
D. Communication breakdown

34. **"Jurassic Park," a groundbreaking film in terms of visual effects and computer-generated imagery, was released in which year?**
A. 1990
B. 1993
C. 1995
D. 1997

35. **In 1997, which Asian financial crisis affected economies worldwide and led to a devaluation of several Asian currencies?**
A. The Japanese financial crisis
B. The Southeast Asian financial crisis
C. The Indian financial crisis
D. The Chinese financial crisis

36. **The first Chechen War, a conflict between the Russian Federation and the Chechen Republic of Ichkeria, began in 1994 and ended in which year?**
A. 1996
B. 1998
C. 2000

D. 2002

37. **The sitcom "Friends," which became one of the most popular TV shows of the 1990s, was set in which city?**
A. Los Angeles
B. New York City
C. Chicago
D. San Francisco

38. **In 1994, a major genocide occurred in Rwanda. Which two ethnic groups were primarily involved in the conflict?**
A. Hutu and Tutsi
B. Zulu and Xhosa
C. Somali and Oromo
D. Ashanti and Yoruba

39. **In the 1990s, a movement and musical style originating in Seattle became popular. This style is known as what?**
A. Punk
B. Grunge
C. Heavy Metal
D. Hip Hop

40. **The popular children's book series "Goosebumps," written by R.L. Stine, was first published in which year?**
A. 1992
B. 1994
C. 1996
D. 1998

41.     In 1991, the first **Gulf War** was fought in response to Iraq's invasion of which country?
A. Iran
B. Saudi Arabia
C. Kuwait
D. Qatar

42.     The **1992 Summer Olympics**, notable for the participation of professional basketball players from the **NBA**, were held in which city?
A. Barcelona
B. Atlanta
C. Seoul
D. Sydney

43.     The **World Trade Organization (WTO)**, established in 1995, replaced which previous international organization?
A. The United Nations Conference on Trade and Development
B. The International Monetary Fund
C. The General Agreement on Tariffs and Trade
D. The World Bank

44.     In 1992, who became the first Canadian woman to be inducted into the **Rock and Roll Hall of Fame?**
A. Joni Mitchell
B. Celine Dion
C. Shania Twain
D. Alanis Morissette

45. **Which science fiction television series created by Chris Carter, centered around FBI agents investigating unexplained phenomena and alien conspiracies, debuted in 1993?**
A. Star Trek: The Next Generation
B. Babylon 5
C. The X-Files
D. Stargate SG-1

46. **The famous chess match between world champion Garry Kasparov and the IBM computer Deep Blue took place in which year?**
A. 1996
B. 1997
C. 1999
D. 2000

47. **In 1998, which two companies merged in what was at the time the largest merger in history, valued at over $160 billion?**
A. Microsoft and Nokia
B. Exxon and Mobil
C. AOL and Time Warner
D. Vodafone and Mannesmann

48. **The 1997 Kyoto Protocol, an international treaty on climate change, aimed to reduce emissions of what?**
A. Plastic waste
B. Nuclear waste
C. Greenhouse gases

D. Ozone-depleting substances

49.      **In 1992, Bill Clinton was elected as the 42nd President of the United States, defeating incumbent President George H.W. Bush. What state was Clinton the governor of before his presidency?**
A. Arkansas
B. Texas
C. Tennessee
D. Alabama

50.      **"Braveheart," a film directed by and starring Mel Gibson, won the Academy Award for Best Picture in which year?**
A. 1995
B. 1996
C. 1997
D. 1998

51.      **The first Harry Potter book, "Harry Potter and the Philosopher's Stone" (later renamed "Sorcerer's Stone" in the U.S.), was published in which year?**
A. 1997
B. 1998
C. 1999
D. 2000

52.      **The 1990s saw the rise of the Internet and personal computing. Which company introduced the iMac in 1998?**
A. Microsoft
B. IBM

C. Dell

D. Apple

53.    **In 1995, a sarin gas attack in a subway system shocked the world. In which city did this terrorist act occur?**

A. New York City

B. London

C. Tokyo

D. Paris

54.    **In 1991, the Persian Gulf War was fought to expel Iraqi forces from which country?**

A. Iran

B. Saudi Arabia

C. Kuwait

D. Qatar

55.    **"Titanic," a film directed by James Cameron, became one of the highest-grossing films ever upon its release in which year?**

A. 1995

B. 1997

C. 1999

D. 2000

56.    **The Oslo Accords, an attempt to resolve the Israeli-Palestinian conflict, were signed in which year?**

A. 1991

B. 1993

C. 1995

D. 1997

57. **In 1999, the European Union introduced a new currency, the Euro, which replaced the national currencies of many member states. Which of the following countries did not initially adopt the Euro?**
A. Germany
B. France
C. Spain
D. United Kingdom

58. **The 1990s grunge movement was characterized by its raw sound and was primarily associated with bands from which city?**
A. Los Angeles
B. New York City
C. Seattle
D. San Francisco

59. **In 1996, a sheep named Dolly made headlines as the first successful cloning of a mammal from an adult cell. Where did this scientific breakthrough occur?**
A. United States
B. United Kingdom
C. Switzerland
D. Japan

60. **The term "ethnic cleansing" became widely known during the 1990s due to conflicts in which region?**
A. Middle East

B. Southeast Asia

C. Balkans

D. Central Africa

61.     **The 1999 movie "The Matrix," known for its groundbreaking special effects, was directed by which sibling duo?**

A. The Coen Brothers

B. The Farrelly Brothers

C. The Wachowskis

D. The Russo Brothers

62.     **In 1996, IBM's Deep Blue became the first computer to win a chess game against a reigning world champion under standard chess tournament conditions. Who was the world champion?**

A. Anatoly Karpov

B. Garry Kasparov

C. Bobby Fischer

D. Magnus Carlsen

63.     **The 1994 FIFA World Cup, hosted by the United States, was won by which country?**

A. Brazil

B. Italy

C. Germany

D. Argentina

64.     **"Friends," a popular TV sitcom that started in the 1990s, revolves around a group of friends living in which city?**

A. Los Angeles

B. New York City
C. Chicago
D. San Francisco

65.     **In 1997, the United Kingdom handed Hong Kong back to China, ending over 150 years of British control. This event is known as what?**
A. The Hong Kong Handover
B. The Sino-British Exchange
C. The Hong Kong Transition
D. The Eastern Agreement

66.     **The popular children's television show "Teletubbies" debuted in 1997 in which country?**
A. United States
B. Australia
C. Canada
D. United Kingdom

67.     **In 1992, the largest shopping mall in the United States, the Mall of America, opened in which state?**
A. California
B. Texas
C. Minnesota
D. New York

68.     **"Schindler's List," a film about a German businessman who saved the lives of more than a thousand Polish-Jewish refugees during the Holocaust, was directed by which filmmaker?**

A. Martin Scorsese
B. Steven Spielberg
C. Francis Ford Coppola
D. Ridley Scott

69.	**The Oslo Accords, aimed at achieving a peace treaty between Israel and the Palestine Liberation Organization (PLO), were signed in which year?**
A. 1990
B. 1992
C. 1993
D. 1995

70.	**In 1998, which tech giants merged in a deal valued at $37 billion, one of the largest mergers in tech history at the time?**
A. Microsoft and LinkedIn
B. AOL and Time Warner
C. Compaq and Hewlett-Packard
D. Google and YouTube

71.	**The programming language Java, now widely used in software development, was developed by which company in the mid-1990s?**
A. Microsoft
B. Apple
C. IBM
D. Sun Microsystems

72.	**In 1999, the Euro currency was introduced and adopted by several European Union countries. Which of the**

following was not one of the first countries to adopt the Euro?
A. France
B. Germany
C. Italy
D. United Kingdom

73.      **The 1991 Gulf War, triggered by Iraq's invasion of Kuwait, saw a large coalition force led by which country?**
A. The United Kingdom
B. The United States
C. Saudi Arabia
D. Russia

74.      **"Saving Private Ryan," a war film set during World War II and known for its realistic portrayal of the D-Day invasion, was released in which year?**
A. 1996
B. 1998
C. 2000
D. 2002

75.      **The Columbine High School massacre, one of the deadliest school shootings in U.S. history, occurred in which state in 1999?**
A. California
B. Texas
C. Colorado
D. Florida

76.    **In 1991, the first website was created and went online. It was developed at CERN by Tim Berners-Lee. What was the main purpose of this website?**
A. To provide information about the World Wide Web project itself
B. To offer a search engine for the internet
C. To connect social media users
D. To sell products online

77.    **Which U.S. city hosted the Summer Olympics in 1996?**
A. Atlanta
B. Los Angeles
C. New York
D. Chicago

78.    **The 1990s was the decade of the boy band. Which of these bands was not formed in the 1990s?**
A. Backstreet Boys
B. NSYNC
C. Boyz II Men
D. New Kids on the Block

79.    **In 1992, which hurricane caused massive destruction in Florida, becoming one of the costliest hurricanes in U.S. history at the time?**
A. Hurricane Katrina
B. Hurricane Sandy
C. Hurricane Andrew
D. Hurricane Irene

80. The first cloned mammal, **Dolly the sheep, was cloned in 1996. In which country did this scientific breakthrough occur?**
A. United States
B. Scotland
C. Germany
D. Japan

81. **In 1994, Nelson Mandela became the first black President of South Africa. He was a member of which political party?**
A. African National Congress
B. Pan Africanist Congress
C. Democratic Alliance
D. Inkatha Freedom Party

82. **In 1990, the reunification of Germany occurred following the fall of the Berlin Wall. East and West Germany were officially united on what date?**
A. October 3, 1990
B. November 9, 1990
C. January 1, 1990
D. December 25, 1990

83. **The "Battle of Seattle" in 1999 was a large-scale protest against a meeting of which organization?**
A. The United Nations
B. The World Trade Organization
C. The International Monetary Fund
D. The World Bank

84. **Which 1997 film, starring Leonardo DiCaprio and Kate Winslet, became the highest-grossing film at the time?**
A. Titanic
B. Romeo + Juliet
C. The Beach
D. Catch Me If You Can

85. **In 1990, the Hubble Space Telescope was launched into space. However, it faced a significant issue with its main mirror. What was the problem?**
A. It was broken during launch
B. It had a spherical aberration
C. It was misaligned
D. It failed to deploy

86. **In 1996, which musician released the influential album "Jagged Little Pill"?**
A. Sheryl Crow
B. Alanis Morissette
C. Fiona Apple
D. Courtney Love

87. **The first successful trial of Dolly the sheep, the first mammal cloned from an adult cell, was announced in 1997. Where did this scientific breakthrough take place?**
A. United States
B. United Kingdom
C. Australia
D. Germany

88.    In 1998, which search engine company was founded by Larry Page and Sergey Brin while they were Ph.D. students at Stanford University?

A. Yahoo

B. Bing

C. Google

D. Ask Jeeves

89.    The Channel Tunnel, or "Chunnel," linking France and the United Kingdom, was completed and opened in which year?

A. 1990

B. 1992

C. 1994

D. 1996

90.    Which international treaty, signed in 1997, was aimed at reducing greenhouse gas emissions to fight global warming?

A. The Paris Agreement

B. The Kyoto Protocol

C. The Montreal Protocol

D. The Copenhagen Accord

91.    In 1998, the International Space Station (ISS) began construction. This project is a multinational collaborative effort involving how many countries?

A. 5

B. 10

C. 15

D. 20

92.     The popular sitcom "Seinfeld," known for its portrayal of everyday life, aired its final episode in which year?
A. 1997
B. 1998
C. 1999
D. 2000

93.     **In 1997, a chess match between Garry Kasparov and the IBM computer Deep Blue resulted in a win for whom?**
A. Garry Kasparov
B. Deep Blue
C. The match ended in a draw
D. The match was inconclusive

94.     **The first book in the "Harry Potter" series by J.K. Rowling was published in 1997. What is the title of this book?**
A. Harry Potter and the Chamber of Secrets
B. Harry Potter and the Goblet of Fire
C. Harry Potter and the Philosopher's Stone
D. Harry Potter and the Prisoner of Azkaban

95.     **The 1994 Northridge earthquake, one of the costliest natural disasters in U.S. history at the time, occurred in which state?**
A. California
B. Florida
C. New York
D. Texas

96.    **In 1992, the largest shopping mall in America, the Mall of America, opened in which state?**
A. California
B. New York
C. Texas
D. Minnesota

97.    **"The Lion King," a popular Disney animated film released in the 1990s, came out in which year?**
A. 1992
B. 1994
C. 1996
D. 1998

98.    **The cloning of Dolly the sheep in 1996 was a significant scientific breakthrough. Dolly was cloned from a cell taken from which part of the body?**
A. Ear
B. Tail
C. Heart
D. Liver

99.    **The 1992 Earth Summit, a major United Nations conference focusing on environmental and sustainable development, was held in which city?**
A. New York
B. Geneva
C. Rio de Janeiro
D. Tokyo

100.    **In the 1990s, the term 'BRICS' was coined to refer to the emerging economies of Brazil, Russia, India, China, and South Africa. Who is credited with coining this term?**
A. Kofi Annan
B. Jim O'Neill
C. Christine Lagarde
D. Ban Ki-moon

# Memories from the 1990s

*Your stories and experiences from the 1990s:*

# The 1990s Word Search Challenge

```
X  M  R  Z  Q  A  G  T  E  X  V  F  Z  X  B
S  M  O  F  K  U  A  G  E  T  I  L  G  L  C
O  G  P  C  L  M  N  I  S  N  S  U  W  M  Q
T  H  L  F  T  U  A  D  S  M  R  S  W  P  N
J  I  W  K  R  O  N  R  P  O  K  E  M  O  N
E  A  T  G  P  E  D  N  P  O  D  R  T  O  Z
R  L  H  A  I  J  E  O  N  I  R  V  A  N  A
L  E  B  R  N  A  L  T  O  Z  J  J  D  W  I
N  D  F  K  L  I  S  N  R  T  X  D  H  A  A
G  N  S  Z  J  F  C  I  U  H  U  E  T  D  G
I  A  O  E  Z  I  H  L  E  M  U  F  X  Q  O
U  M  L  Y  K  V  B  C  N  J  Y  B  W  C  O
I  H  C  T  O  G  A  M  A  T  R  Z  B  J  G
P  L  A  Y  S  T  A  T  I  O  N  G  V  L  L
K  R  A  P  C  I  S  S  A  R  U  J  B  N  E
```

| Clinton | Nirvana | GulfWar | DVD |
| --- | --- | --- | --- |
| Euro | Tamagotchi | JurassicPark | Google |
| Grunge | Dotcom | PlayStation | Mandela |
| Internet | FriendsTV | Titanic | Pokemon |

# Answer Key Section 1: The 1950s

| 1950s | A | B | C | D |
|---|---|---|---|---|
| 1 | ● | | | |
| 2 | ● | | | |
| 3 | ● | | | |
| 4 | | ● | | |
| 5 | | ● | | |
| 6 | | ● | | |
| 7 | | | ● | |
| 8 | | ● | | |
| 9 | | | | ● |
| 10 | | ● | | |
| 11 | | | ● | |
| 12 | | | | ● |
| 13 | | ● | | |
| 14 | | | ● | |
| 15 | | ● | | |
| 16 | ● | | | |
| 17 | | | ● | |
| 18 | | | | ● |
| 19 | | | ● | |
| 20 | | ● | | |
| 21 | | | ● | |
| 22 | | ● | | |
| 23 | | | | ● |
| 24 | | | ● | |
| 25 | | ● | | |

| 1950s | A | B | C | D |
|---|---|---|---|---|
| 26 | | | | ● |
| 27 | ● | | | |
| 28 | | | ● | |
| 29 | | ● | | |
| 30 | | ● | | |
| 31 | | ● | | |
| 32 | | ● | | |
| 33 | | | | ● |
| 34 | | | ● | |
| 35 | | | ● | |
| 36 | | ● | | |
| 37 | | | ● | |
| 38 | | | | ● |
| 39 | ● | | | |
| 40 | ● | | | |
| 41 | | | ● | |
| 42 | | ● | | |
| 43 | | ● | | |
| 44 | | ● | | |
| 45 | | ● | | |
| 46 | | | ● | |
| 47 | ● | | | |
| 48 | | ● | | |
| 49 | | ● | | |
| 50 | | | ● | |

| 1950s | A | B | C | D |
|---|---|---|---|---|
| 51 | | ● | | |
| 52 | | | ● | |
| 53 | | ● | | |
| 54 | ● | | | |
| 55 | | | ● | |
| 56 | | | | ● |
| 57 | | | ● | |
| 58 | | | | ● |
| 59 | | | ● | |
| 60 | | | | ● |
| 61 | | ● | | |
| 62 | ● | | | |
| 63 | | | ● | |
| 64 | ● | | | |
| 65 | | | ● | |
| 66 | | ● | | |
| 67 | | ● | | |
| 68 | | ● | | |
| 69 | | ● | | |
| 70 | | | ● | |
| 71 | | | | ● |
| 72 | | | | ● |
| 73 | | ● | | |
| 74 | ● | | | |
| 75 | | ● | | |

| 1950s | A | B | C | D |
|---|---|---|---|---|
| 76 | | | ● | |
| 77 | | ● | | |
| 78 | | ● | | |
| 79 | | | ● | |
| 80 | | ● | | |
| 81 | | | ● | |
| 82 | | | | ● |
| 83 | | | ● | |
| 84 | | ● | | |
| 85 | | | ● | |
| 86 | | | ● | |
| 87 | | | | ● |
| 88 | | | | ● |
| 89 | | ● | | |
| 90 | | | ● | |
| 91 | ● | | | |
| 92 | | ● | | |
| 93 | | | ● | |
| 94 | | ● | | |
| 95 | | | ● | |
| 96 | | | | ● |
| 97 | | | ● | |
| 98 | | | ● | |
| 99 | | | ● | |
| 100 | | | ● | |

# Answer Key Section 2: The 1960s

| 1960s | A | B | C | D |
|---|---|---|---|---|
| 1 | ● | | | |
| 2 | | ● | | |
| 3 | | | ● | |
| 4 | | ● | | |
| 5 | | | ● | |
| 6 | | | ● | |
| 7 | ● | | | |
| 8 | | ● | | |
| 9 | | ● | | |
| 10 | | | ● | |
| 11 | | ● | | |
| 12 | | ● | | |
| 13 | | | | ● |
| 14 | | | ● | |
| 15 | ● | | | |
| 16 | | ● | | |
| 17 | | ● | | |
| 18 | | | | ● |
| 19 | | | ● | |
| 20 | | | | ● |
| 21 | | | ● | |
| 22 | ● | | | |
| 23 | ● | | | |
| 24 | | | ● | |
| 25 | | ● | | |

| 1960s | A | B | C | D |
|---|---|---|---|---|
| 26 | ● | | | |
| 27 | | | ● | |
| 28 | | ● | | |
| 29 | | | ● | |
| 30 | | ● | | |
| 31 | | | ● | |
| 32 | | ● | | |
| 33 | | | ● | |
| 34 | | | | ● |
| 35 | ● | | | |
| 36 | | | ● | |
| 37 | | | ● | |
| 38 | | | ● | |
| 39 | | | | ● |
| 40 | ● | | | |
| 41 | | | ● | |
| 42 | | | ● | |
| 43 | | | ● | |
| 44 | ● | | | |
| 45 | | | ● | |
| 46 | ● | | | |
| 47 | | | ● | |
| 48 | | | ● | |
| 49 | | | ● | |
| 50 | ● | | | |

| 1960s | A | B | C | D |
|---|---|---|---|---|
| 51 | ● | | | |
| 52 | | ● | | |
| 53 | ● | | | |
| 54 | | | | ● |
| 55 | | | | ● |
| 56 | | | ● | |
| 57 | | | ● | |
| 58 | | | | ● |
| 59 | | | ● | |
| 60 | | | ● | |
| 61 | | | ● | |
| 62 | | | ● | |
| 63 | | | ● | |
| 64 | | ● | | |
| 65 | | | ● | |
| 66 | | | | ● |
| 67 | | | ● | |
| 68 | | ● | | |
| 69 | | | ● | |
| 70 | | | ● | |
| 71 | | | | ● |
| 72 | | ● | | |
| 73 | | ● | | |
| 74 | ● | | | |
| 75 | | | | ● |

| 1960s | A | B | C | D |
|---|---|---|---|---|
| 76 | | ● | | |
| 77 | | | ● | |
| 78 | | ● | | |
| 79 | | | ● | |
| 80 | | | ● | |
| 81 | | | | ● |
| 82 | | | ● | |
| 83 | | | ● | |
| 84 | | ● | | |
| 85 | | ● | | |
| 86 | | | ● | |
| 87 | | | ● | |
| 88 | ● | | | |
| 89 | | ● | | |
| 90 | | | ● | |
| 91 | | ● | | |
| 92 | | ● | | |
| 93 | | | ● | |
| 94 | | ● | | |
| 95 | | ● | | |
| 96 | | | ● | |
| 97 | | | ● | |
| 98 | | ● | | |
| 99 | | ● | | |
| 100 | | | | ● |

# Answer Key Section 3: The 1970s

| 1970s | A | B | C | D |
|---|---|---|---|---|
| 1 | ● | | | |
| 2 | | | ● | |
| 3 | | ● | | |
| 4 | ● | | | |
| 5 | | | | ● |
| 6 | ● | | | |
| 7 | | | ● | |
| 8 | | ● | | |
| 9 | | | ● | |
| 10 | | | ● | |
| 11 | ● | | | |
| 12 | | | ● | |
| 13 | | ● | | |
| 14 | | ● | | |
| 15 | | ● | | |
| 16 | ● | | | |
| 17 | | | ● | |
| 18 | | ● | | |
| 19 | | | ● | |
| 20 | | ● | | |
| 21 | | ● | | |
| 22 | | ● | | |
| 23 | | ● | | |
| 24 | ● | | | |
| 25 | | | ● | |

| 1970s | A | B | C | D |
|---|---|---|---|---|
| 26 | ● | | | |
| 27 | | | | ● |
| 28 | | ● | | |
| 29 | | ● | | |
| 30 | | ● | | |
| 31 | ● | | | |
| 32 | | ● | | |
| 33 | ● | | | |
| 34 | | ● | | |
| 35 | | | ● | |
| 36 | | | ● | |
| 37 | | | ● | |
| 38 | | ● | | |
| 39 | | | | ● |
| 40 | | | ● | |
| 41 | | ● | | |
| 42 | | | ● | |
| 43 | | ● | | |
| 44 | | | ● | |
| 45 | ● | | | |
| 46 | | | | ● |
| 47 | | | ● | |
| 48 | | ● | | |
| 49 | | | | ● |
| 50 | ● | | | |

| 1970s | A | B | C | D |
|---|---|---|---|---|
| 51 | | | ● | |
| 52 | | | ● | |
| 53 | ● | | | |
| 54 | | | ● | |
| 55 | | | | ● |
| 56 | | | ● | |
| 57 | | ● | | |
| 58 | ● | | | |
| 59 | | ● | | |
| 60 | | | ● | |
| 61 | ● | | | |
| 62 | | | ● | |
| 63 | | | ● | |
| 64 | ● | | | |
| 65 | ● | | | |
| 66 | | ● | | |
| 67 | | ● | | |
| 68 | ● | | | |
| 69 | ● | | | |
| 70 | | | ● | |
| 71 | | | ● | |
| 72 | | ● | | |
| 73 | | | ● | |
| 74 | ● | | | |
| 75 | ● | ● | | |

| 1970s | A | B | C | D |
|---|---|---|---|---|
| 76 | | | ● | |
| 77 | | ● | | |
| 78 | | | | ● |
| 79 | | | ● | |
| 80 | | | ● | |
| 81 | | ● | | |
| 82 | | | ● | |
| 83 | | ● | | |
| 84 | | | | ● |
| 85 | ● | | | |
| 86 | | ● | | |
| 87 | | ● | | |
| 88 | | | | ● |
| 89 | | | ● | |
| 90 | | ● | | |
| 91 | ● | | | |
| 92 | | ● | | |
| 93 | ● | | | |
| 94 | | | ● | |
| 95 | ● | | | |
| 96 | ● | | | |
| 97 | | | ● | |
| 98 | | | ● | |
| 99 | | ● | | |
| 100 | | | ● | |

# Answer Key Section 4: The 1980s

| 1980s | A | B | C | D |
|---|---|---|---|---|
| 1 | | | ● | |
| 2 | ● | | | |
| 3 | | ● | | |
| 4 | | ● | | |
| 5 | ● | | | |
| 6 | ● | | | |
| 7 | | ● | | |
| 8 | | | ● | |
| 9 | | | ● | |
| 10 | | ● | | |
| 11 | | | ● | |
| 12 | | | ● | |
| 13 | | ● | | |
| 14 | ● | | | |
| 15 | | | ● | |
| 16 | | | ● | |
| 17 | ● | | | |
| 18 | ● | | | |
| 19 | | | ● | |
| 20 | | | ● | |
| 21 | ● | | | |
| 22 | ● | | | |
| 23 | ● | | | |
| 24 | | | ● | |
| 25 | | ● | | |

| 1980s | A | B | C | D |
|---|---|---|---|---|
| 26 | | | ● | |
| 27 | | | ● | |
| 28 | ● | | | |
| 29 | ● | | | |
| 30 | | | | ● |
| 31 | | | ● | |
| 32 | | ● | | |
| 33 | | ● | | |
| 34 | | | ● | |
| 35 | | | ● | |
| 36 | | | | ● |
| 37 | | ● | | |
| 38 | | | | ● |
| 39 | | ● | | |
| 40 | ● | | | |
| 41 | | ● | | |
| 42 | | | ● | |
| 43 | | ● | | |
| 44 | | | ● | |
| 45 | ● | | | |
| 46 | | | ● | |
| 47 | | ● | | |
| 48 | | | ● | |
| 49 | | ● | | |
| 50 | ● | | | |

| 1980s | A | B | C | D |
|---|---|---|---|---|
| 51 | ● | | | |
| 52 | | ● | | |
| 53 | ● | | | |
| 54 | ● | | | |
| 55 | | ● | | |
| 56 | ● | | | |
| 57 | ● | | | |
| 58 | | ● | | |
| 59 | ● | | | |
| 60 | ● | | | |
| 61 | | | ● | |
| 62 | | | ● | |
| 63 | | ● | | |
| 64 | ● | | | |
| 65 | | | ● | |
| 66 | | ● | | |
| 67 | | ● | | |
| 68 | | | ● | |
| 69 | ● | | | |
| 70 | ● | | | |
| 71 | | | ● | |
| 72 | ● | | | |
| 73 | | | ● | |
| 74 | | | ● | |
| 75 | | ● | | |

| 1980s | A | B | C | D |
|---|---|---|---|---|
| 76 | | | ● | |
| 77 | | | ● | |
| 78 | | ● | | |
| 79 | | | | ● |
| 80 | | | ● | |
| 81 | | ● | | |
| 82 | | | ● | |
| 83 | | | | ● |
| 84 | ● | | | |
| 85 | | ● | | |
| 86 | ● | | | |
| 87 | | ● | | |
| 88 | ● | | | |
| 89 | ● | | | |
| 90 | | | ● | |
| 91 | | ● | | |
| 92 | | ● | | |
| 93 | | ● | | |
| 94 | | | ● | |
| 95 | | ● | | |
| 96 | | ● | | |
| 97 | ● | | | |
| 98 | ● | | | |
| 99 | ● | | | |
| 100 | | ● | | |

# Answer Key Section 5: The 1990s

| 1990s | A | B | C | D |
|---|---|---|---|---|
| 1 | | | ● | |
| 2 | | | ● | |
| 3 | | | ● | |
| 4 | | | ● | |
| 5 | | ● | | |
| 6 | | ● | | |
| 7 | ● | | | |
| 8 | | ● | | |
| 9 | ● | | | |
| 10 | | | ● | |
| 11 | | ● | | |
| 12 | | ● | | |
| 13 | | ● | | |
| 14 | | | ● | |
| 15 | | | ● | |
| 16 | | | ● | |
| 17 | | ● | | |
| 18 | | | ● | |
| 19 | ● | | | |
| 20 | | | | ● |
| 21 | ● | | | |
| 22 | | | ● | |
| 23 | | | ● | |
| 24 | | | ● | |
| 25 | | | ● | |

| 1990s | A | B | C | D |
|---|---|---|---|---|
| 26 | ● | | | |
| 27 | | ● | | |
| 28 | ● | | | |
| 29 | | | ● | |
| 30 | | ● | | |
| 31 | | | ● | |
| 32 | ● | | | |
| 33 | ● | | | |
| 34 | | ● | | |
| 35 | | ● | | |
| 36 | ● | | | |
| 37 | | ● | | |
| 38 | ● | | | |
| 39 | | ● | | |
| 40 | ● | | | |
| 41 | | | ● | |
| 42 | ● | | | |
| 43 | | | ● | |
| 44 | ● | | | |
| 45 | | | ● | |
| 46 | | ● | | |
| 47 | | ● | | |
| 48 | | | ● | |
| 49 | ● | | | |
| 50 | ● | | | |

| 1990s | A | B | C | D |
|---|---|---|---|---|
| 51 | ● | | | |
| 52 | | | | ● |
| 53 | | ● | | |
| 54 | | ● | | |
| 55 | | ● | | |
| 56 | | ● | | |
| 57 | | | | ● |
| 58 | | ● | | |
| 59 | | ● | | |
| 60 | | | ● | |
| 61 | | | ● | |
| 62 | | ● | | |
| 63 | ● | | | |
| 64 | | ● | | |
| 65 | ● | | | |
| 66 | | | | ● |
| 67 | | | ● | |
| 68 | | ● | | |
| 69 | | | ● | |
| 70 | | | ● | |
| 71 | | | | ● |
| 72 | | | | ● |
| 73 | | ● | | |
| 74 | | ● | | |
| 75 | | | ● | |

| 1990s | A | B | C | D |
|---|---|---|---|---|
| 76 | ● | | | |
| 77 | ● | | | |
| 78 | | | | ● |
| 79 | | | ● | |
| 80 | | ● | | |
| 81 | ● | | | |
| 82 | ● | | | |
| 83 | | ● | | |
| 84 | ● | | | |
| 85 | | ● | | |
| 86 | | ● | | |
| 87 | | ● | | |
| 88 | | | ● | |
| 89 | | | ● | |
| 90 | | ● | | |
| 91 | | | ● | |
| 92 | | ● | | |
| 93 | | ● | | |
| 94 | | | ● | |
| 95 | ● | | | |
| 96 | | | | ● |
| 97 | | ● | | |
| 98 | ● | | | |
| 99 | | | ● | |
| 100 | | ● | | |